WOMEN WORK PARTICIPATION IN PUBLIC AND PRIVATE SECTOR ORGANISATIONS

WOMEN WORK PARTICIPATION IN PUBLIC AND PRIVATE SECTOR ORGANISATIONS

L. THILAGARANI

SERIALS PUBLICATIONS
NEW DELHI

First Published-2010

ISBN: 978-81-8387-372-7

Published by

SERIALS PUBLICATIONS
4830/24, Prahlad Street, Ansari Road
Darya Ganj, New Delhi-110002 (India)
Phone : 23245225 Fax : 91-11-23272135
E-mail: serials@sify.com

CONTENTS

ACKNOWLEDGEMENT

At the outset, I wish to record my deep gratitude to my research guide **Dr.V. Dhulasi Birundha,** Professor and Head, Department of Environmental Economics, School of Economics, Madurai Kamaraj University, Madurai, whose discerning eye pervaded the whole of this thesis for her scholarly guidance that instilled infectious confidence, constructive criticism that kindled fresh thinking and her profound affection towards me.

I happily record at this juncture, here my abiding gratitude to professors, **Dr. G. Subramaniyan** and **Dr. R. Haridoss**, former Head & Co-ordinators, School of Economics, Madurai Kamaraj University, Madurai, for their valuable suggestions and encouragement.

I am deeply indebted to **Dr. E. Thirumalai Kumarasamy**, former Head of the Department of Economics, The M.D.T. Hindu College, Tirunelveli, for his guidance, valuable suggestions and encouragement.

My sincere thanks to **Rev. Sister Vittaline Mary, Rev. Sister Beatina Mary** and **Rev. Sister Avelin Mary,** former Principals, St. Mary's College, Thoothukudi, for their encouragement throughout the study.

My thanks to **Rev. Sister Arulananda Mary,** Principal, St. Mary's College, Thoothukudi, for her encouragement.

My thanks are due to **Rev. Sister Vasanthi Mary**, Librarian, St. Mary's College, Thoothukudi, in a special way for the excellent library facilities that I could avail through her.

I am also grateful to **Mr. N. Murugesan**, Sri Balaji Computers, Palkalai Nagar, Madurai, for his ceaseless efforts in the processing and the neat printing of my thesis work.

Last, but not least I ought to acknowledge the forbearance and the sacrifices of my ever loving husband, family members and my friends whose blessings have been the perennial sources of strength to me all through my endeavours.

1

INTRODUCTION

INTRODUCTION

A working woman has a more interesting life than one who does not work and there is also the charm of a pay-pocket- but she often has to pay a heavy price for all this.

– Manjit Bhatia

"To awaken the people, it is the women who must be awakened. Once she is on the move, the family moves, the village moves and the nation moves"

– Jawaharlal Nehru

Importance of Women - As a Human Resource

Women who constitute half of the world's population are not fully harnessed as a human resource. Any society cannot go ahead if 50 per cent of the population do not participate in its developmental activities. Indira Gandhi, the former Prime Minister of India observed that neglect of women would be criminal since humanity had been deprived of half of the energy and creative talents. Right through history, in all religions and cultures women have been assigned a secondary status. (Shakuntala Balaraman, 1986).

The world wars proved to be a turning point in the history of mankind. The participation of women in the work force started increasing since then. This trend is observed in developing nations (Kakpana Sharma, 1988).

In tune with the world wide trend, Indian women are marching towards self-development. In India, women played a secondary role for centuries together. During the colonial rule, women lived a miserable and horrible life in diverse situations (Krishnamurthy, 1990).

Mahatma Gandhi, Father of Indian Nation helped women to find a new dignity in public life, a new place in the national mainstream, a new confidence and a consciousness that they could act against oppression (Madhu Kishwar, 1985).

The socio-economic changes that were set in motion in India after independence provided women with better educational and employment opportunities. Besides, a series of laws such as the Special Marriage Act 1954, the Hindu marriage Act 1955, Equal Remuneration Act 1976 passed by the government of India helped to improve the lot of women. Today educated Indian women have made a landmark in the non-conventional fields like consultancy, marketing, advertising, garment exporting, interior decoration, beauty parlours, road and building construction. Women have started coming forward in considerable number in certain spheres of higher category jobs like civil service, judiciary, foreign service, medicine and architecture. In organised sectors like banking, insurance, communication and air transport women's share in employment has recently doubled over the decade and government's intervention played an important role in this regard (Nirmala Banerjee, 1989).

ROLE OF WOMEN

Women are at the heart of development. They control most of the non-money economy (subsistence agriculture, bearing and raring children, domestic labour) and take an important part in the money economy (trading, the 'informal sector', wage employment). Everywhere in the world women have two jobs-around the home and outside it.

Women are half the world's population, receive one-tenth of the world's income, account for two-thirds of the world's working hours, and own only one-hundredth of the world's property. The process of industrialisation, urbanisation and the increased educational and employment opportunities for women have brought about changes in the traditional attitudes and values of urban women in India.

The role of women in our society even as career women, not to speak of householders is not insignificant. They have played a significant role in the socio - economic and political development of our country. The old order which confined women to the home as servants, and helpers to their men folk, is being replaced now by a new one in which women increasingly undertake to fulfil many roles, within the home as wives, mothers and home makers and outside it, as partners and co-workers of men in all types of enterprises. The few fortunate women who have the benefits of higher education seem to be quite obvious of their immense responsibilities for the emancipation of the women in the country side and of the working and middle class families in urban areas. The production side of women's work at home is gradually decreasing leading to a reduction of woman's role at home. Women perceive more and more clearly that if they really want to contribute to the welfare of their family and society the most effective way is to go out of home and earn money (Sumit Gupta and Mukta Gupta, 1989).

Besides, soaring prices and rise in materialism make man work against time in his attempt to survive in the fast changing society, and also to accumulate more and more goods. If he cannot do it alone, his wife has to provide more, either by bringing in a fat dowry or by going out to work. Thus we have a working woman (Kalpana Roy, 1999).

Today, the state has accepted women's empowerment, and women as active agents participating in their own development. Most of the countries now recognise the need for gender justice and equality. Women can change the nature of power rather than power change the nature of women. Women try to devote most of their time for maintaining their living standard with the help of earnings through employment in urban areas.

Emancipation of women is one of the indicators of economic development and social changes. The position of women in a society is an index of its level of civilisation. Women constitute one half of the population, that is one half of the country's human resources. Apart from the fact that they constitute one half of the country's 'man power', women play an important role in shaping the personalities of the nations' young human resources (Rani Moses, 1992).

The position of women has changed not only in the sphere of marriage and family but also in the spheres of education, employment and political life. Women's employment has an important role in women's empowerment. Employing of women particularly in the organised sector ensures better living conditions for herself and her family.

If women are to empower themselves they have to be provided with wholesome opportunities and rights, access to basic civic amenities, right to education, right to earn a livelihood, right to equal wages, right to question, and fight justice, right to decision-making to live way they want, protection against violence and injustice to them. They need the strength to free themselves from the oppressive and dependent conditions of living. If national development and women's development have to be purposive and relevant, women have to be equal partners with men and participants. The powerful and deep rooted cultural forces, outdated value systems, discriminatory socialisation process, and oppressive social structural forces that obstruct such an access need to be confronted and reversed.

Women have achieved only limited access to some fields of life. More often they are the implementers of decisions, and not the decision makers for their own cause or any other related cause. She is under constant pressure on the home front and at the work place. The dual roles and responsibilities have resulted in a lot of tension, stress and strain for the women. She is therefore hard pressed in finding time to devote to herself, for her own personality development.

At present, women occupy positions in every field of activity, and command honour and respect similar to men. Thus it may be understood that some of the sociological, economic, and psychological characterization of women have been changed because of education and employment (Murali Manohar, 1989).

Mahatma Gandhi referred to women as the nobler sex. According to him, "If she is weak in striking, she is strong in suffering." In Indian society, the women are visualised in two extreme positions. On the one side, Indian women are celebrated as 'Sakthi', the source of power. On the other side, from the sociological set up, women are being considered as the weaker sex and hence they are left with closed commitments only. In modern society women are said to be equal to men. The actual situation is far from this. The fact is that in modern society women constitute its disadvantaged, if not depressed, section. Irrespective of their social status, women play a very active role in the economic activity either as workers, or as producers of various goods and services or in the domestic side as house-maids. (Sahab Deen Maurya, 1988).

Indian women are patient in nature and do have the capacity to accept every thing. Normally they do have more confidence in the male members of the family. Our culture makes them good subordinates and executors of decisions made by the male members. Moreover in general women are capable of working hard physically on all occasions and mostly at all ages. The women's uplift depends upon two requisites, self-reliance and economic independence. Women's participation in the economic activity is important for their personal advancement and improvement of their status in society. Women must join the labour force of the country on an equal feeling with men and get integrated into the system (Kalpana Roy, 1999).

Strandt said that, 'setting resources into women's hands, integrating women in the wage labour force and securing female rights to enable and empower women for other actions are deemed significant in themselves". Urbanisation, higher education, recognition of talents and abilities and meaningful employment have provided women with new avenues to express and assert themselves. The rural women have been working for a living in the fields alongside of their men. The middle class Indian working women in the cities have stepped out in search of economic gains as well as the fulfillment of their personal hopes and desires. Now, it is admissible even for married women to take up gainful employment. The upper and middle class women are finding a purpose in their lives. Women with education and employment make a mark for themselves in society by the flowering of their personality while retaining their essential womanliness. Their mental orientation is more prepared than a typical household. In the event of working outside, the traditional division of labour has been rearranged to meet the situation (Strandt Kathleen, 1986).

Educational, political, economic and social changes have changed women's status, their roles and way of life. But this could also change their feminine character a little. Indeed they work, but they work for the family that too from economic impulses. They work to support their family. The working women, on the whole, never sought to sublimate or bypass the demands of family life. Rather their homes and families have either come first, or have stood at par with their work.

This role is very significant, as far as the art of maintaining a stable family life and thereby a stable society is concerned.

WOMEN WORK FORCE IN THE LABOUR MARKET

Traditionally women's occupational status has always been closely associated with the home and family. She has only a secondary status because she is economically dependent on her father or husband (Mary Billington, 1978).

In order to improve the status and position of women at home and in the society at large, it is necessary to achieve economic independence for women.

Freedom depends on economic condition even more than political. If a woman is not economically free, without self-employment and self-earnings she will have to depend on her husband or some one else and dependants are never free (Azad Singh Gulab, 1988).

For a woman, an opportunity to productive work is not merely a means to higher income but also to self respect, to the development of her personality and to a sense of participation in the common cause of the society. The low status of women in large segments of Indian society cannot be raised without the opening up of opportunity of independent employment and income.

Economic independence makes women conscious of their rights. By working outside the home and coming into contact with other people they have broadened their outlook and mental horizon (Margret Cormack, 1976).

The image of women in society is fast changing. But it is difficult to define clearly the changing shape of the image. One thing is clear; women are entering the labour force in a large number (Devaki Jain, 1975).

Employment is considered to be an important indicator of women's achievements in the economic sphere. In the organised and industrial sectors employment of women has gone up rapidly. A similar increase could be seen in the unorganised sectors which are outside the reach of public regulation, labour laws and other forms of public control. They are employed in considerable numbers in public services in several countries. They are employed in all services not in the same proportion as that of western countries.

The labour force participation rates particularly of women and teenagers are very sensitive to the general level economic activity. The impact of economic conditions on female labour force participation can take two forms. In times of economic down turn, the wife or other members of the household may enter the labour force to supplement the family income. These additional workers often leave the labour force once the major breadwinner is reemployed on a regular basis. If an employed woman loses her job, and cannot find a new one after a prolonged search, she may become discouraged and leave the labour force. Despite the rapid growth of the female labour force in recent years, women still primarily confine themselves to certain areas and occupations. Women are largely employed in primary sector of the economy. In the secondary and tertiary sectors the female working force is much less as compared to male employed in transport, storage and communications (Subba Rao, 2000).

The phrase 'working women' is generally understood to mean women who take up jobs usually outside the home, the work being mostly of a remunerative nature. The term is however a misnomer in so far as it implies that the housewife is not a 'working woman'. It is indeed surprising that housewives all over the world have not taken exception to this usage (Annupa Gupta, 1971).

Women are employed in all fields. They are shouldering official, family and social burdens. While working in the mixed group, their need to keep up with the status, which can be higher, compared with non-working housewives. Working women can be defined as the employed women ranging from those who are employed in small scale industries and organisation to those who, possess ownership, and authority in organizations, in government, private and quasi-government (Lawrence Marry, 1996).

Working women could be brought under three categories on socio economic basis. The first category includes agricultural workers and those engaged in traditional menial services, construction work and domestic works such as cleaning, cooking and washing.

The second category mostly consists of those women who work in offices or in factories. They can be called the blue-collar women workers.

The third category of women workers are well educated. They are quite well off in life. They have both vertical and horizontal mobility (Gangrade, 1993).

The employment of women under the next three types of industries, electricity, gas and water supply, construction and trade and commerce reveal a downward trend.

These three categories of industries seem to provide the largest avenue of employment to women job - seekers in India. Under the division of transport, storage and, commerce, there was a substantial increase both in the number of workers as well as in their proportion.

The majority of women under these divisions take up the white collar jobs and work as clerks, typists, steno, telephone operators, secretaries, assistants etc. Women workers are preferred in these jobs because of their docile nature. They do not take in general active part in strikes and other trade union activities. This is an important feature of women workers. (Kurukshetra, 1984).

STATEMENT OF THE PROBLEM

The status of women is closely associated with their economic position, which in turn, depends upon their access to productive resources of the country, and the opportunities for participation in economic activities.

"Investing more in women rather than in men leads to proportionately greater development" according to the world bank. A mother's education has a stronger impact on the health of her children than does the father's and income controlled by women is more likely to be spent on household needs than income controlled by ;men. The bank, claims that it will pay special attention to women's participation in economic development under the new policy.

Economic independence for all women with equal opportunity brings out their full potentials as human beings instead of being considered appendages to males.

At present the economic stresses and strains in the modern society brought forth and compelled many women to come out to augment their family income. Their participation in gainful employment is mostly governed by the economic conditions of the family income. The reasons advanced in favour of employment of women were inadequacy of the income of the husbands and also husbands' irresponsibility in family management.

Employment among women from the lower middle class and the poorer socio-economic groups is more common than it is among the elite. Female employment is essential both for national economy as well as for the domestic economy. Employment of women down the decades shows the fact that the impact of unemployment falls more heavily on women than on men. There has been a good deal of discussion in recent years over the question of employment opportunities for women.

Female population in Thoothukudi district is greater in number than the males, but they are more backward in the matter of literacy and employment level than men. Women workers in Thoothukudi district are facing a number of problems on the work spot, which vociferously demand an investigative study.

OBJECTIVES OF THE STUDY

The study has the following objectives:

1. To study the relation between personal characteristics of women work participants and their familial characteristics.
2. To examine the variation in income between public and private sector women employees and assess the women workers contribution towards family income.
3. To analyse and compare the work-family conflict of women employees in public and private sector.
4. To assess the contribution of independent variables to quality of work life of women employees.
5. To analyse the extent to which women work participation empower them through decision-making.
6. To examine the factors which influence the empowerment of working women in public and private sector.

SIGNIFICANCE OF THE STUDY

The study becomes significant because it explains the socio-economic condition of women workers in the organised sector, which will help the government authorities to create new avenues of employment for women. Thus it leads to the gradual uplift of their employment.

Women in position, can act as catalysts in development processes. Handy data on working women are very much needed by planners, administrators and social workers so as to identify their problems and contemplate remedial measures. Some of the research studies have confirmed the point that development of women is a pre-requisite for the overall development of society.

Actually in the first instance the available literature on the working women is inefficient. Even the available literature is virtually on urban and rural working women and further, it is not empirically tested. The present study aims at filling up these gaps to the extent possible.

This may go a long way in guiding the government planners, policy makers, economists and researchers for further research and suggestions regarding this issue. It may give new ideas to the government authorities to implement various developmental programmes to augment their employment status and thus eliminate the unemployment among women in India progressively.

This study also becomes significant as it is possible to assess the overall economic and social status of women in the organised sector, if any, and to suggest some workable solutions also.

LIMITATION OF THE STUDY

The study is restricted to Thoothukudi district where the female working population is sufficient in number for the study purpose and belongs to different sectors. Though a number of governmental organisations are functioning in Thoothukudi district, the researcher has selected women employees working in state and central governments or public sector, and industrial and service departments of the private sector. Because of the industrialised area of Thoothukudi, the researcher studied the industrial units of female workers in the private sector. Hence, the results of the present study are to be viewed with the above limitations.

METHODOLOGY

Designing a suitable methodology and selection of analytical tools are important for a meaningful analysis of any research problem. In this section, an attempt has been made to describe the methodology which includes sampling procedure, period of study, collection of data and tools of analysis.

Sampling Procedure

The present study is confined to women working in organized sector both public and private. In Thoothukudi district the information regarding the list of offices of both public and private sectors was obtained from various sources. Out of 14,642 female workers in Thoothukudi district, a total of 300 sample women working in various offices of both public and private sectors were randomly selected by using random numbers for the purpose of primary data collection. 300 sample women employees were post-stratified into two categories namely public and private sectors. Out of 300 sample women, 163 (54.33 per cent) came under public sector and the remaining 137 (45.67 per cent) came under private sector.

Period of Study

The field survey was carried out from October 2001 to March 2002 for the collection of primary data. The data collection pertains to the financial year 2001-2002.

Collection of Data

The data required for this study have been obtained from primary and secondary sources. First hand data were collected from the field directly through structured comprehensive interview schedule.

Primary data have been collected through personal interview method with a pre-tested schedule which consists of information about the socio-economic characteristics, family characteristics, quality of work life, job satisfaction and the like.

Secondary data related to study have been taken from the District Collector's Office, Thoothukudi, Thoothukudi Municipality, District Employment Office, Employees of State Insurance and different categories of government organizations. The researcher collected information from the Centre for Development Studies (CDS), Trivandrum and also from a few magazines and journals.

HYPOTHESES OF THE STUDY

1. There is no variation in income among the women workers in public and private, central and state, and industry and service sectors.

2. There is no difference in the perception of quality of work life and job satisfaction between women workers in public and private sectors.
3. There is no difference in women empowerment between public and private sector women employees.

TOOLS OF ANALYSIS

In order to examine the relationship between variables, Chi-square test was carried out.

ANOVA was used to test the variation in income among the women workers in public and private sector, Central and State and Industry and Service.

In order to assess the contribution of women employees in family income, a log linear multiple regression model was estimated for public and private sector separately.

To quantify the work-family conflict, quality of work, job satisfaction and empowerment scaling technique has been adopted for the present study.

Two-way ANOVA was carried out to examine whether there was any significant variation in quality of work life and job satisfaction.

Step-wise regression model was computed to assess the contribution of independent variables to quality of work life and empowerment.

The correlation coefficient technique has been used to analyse among the variables of work-family conflict.

One way ANOVA was carried out to examine the variation in empowerment of different sectors.

In order to find out the level of empowerment, arithmetic mean and standard deviation were computed.

To examine the relationship between the level of empowerment and socio-economic factors, Chi-square test was employed.

CONCEPTS

Meaning and Definitions

A clear definition of certain concepts that one might come across in the discussion of the subject would be helpful in the proper understanding of the issues, hence before proceeding with the actual discussion of the problem on hand an attempt is made in this chapter to provide clear meaning and definitions of certain concepts which are used in this study.

Households

A group of persons normally living together and taking food from the same kitchen constitute a household. It usually excludes guests and includes temporary absentees.

Age

Age has been considered as the number of full years completed by women workers at the time of investigation.

Caste

It may be defined as a small and named group of persons characterised by endogamy, hereditary membership and a specific style of life, which also includes the pursuit by tradition of a particular occupation and is usually associated with a more or less distinct ritual status in a hierarchical system.

Religion

A system of beliefs, practices and philosophical values concerned with the definition of the sacred comprehension of life and salvation from the problems of human existence. Religion is essentially an institutionalized or traditional path to salvation.

Family Size

This term means the number of members in a household.

Joint Family

More then one family is sharing food from the same kitchen.

Nuclear Family

It is a family in which the Husband and wife live with any number of their unmarried children.

Separation

When husband and wife do not live together and they have no marital relations that is called separation.

Divorce

It means when either of the party approaches the court or follows some other legal method claiming that relations between them have so much deteriorated that it is impossible for them to lead a married life as husband and wife and a request is made that the marriage be legally dissolved, it inevitably leads to a divorce.

Socio-Economic Background

John.P. Dececo states that socio-eco-background is of special significance to the investigator. He states that "socio-economic background assumes a continuous ranking from high to low on the basis of occupation, education income and so on".

Education

The term 'Education in the widest sense may be held to include the whole process of development through which a human being passes from infancy to maturity, gradually adapting himself to his physical and social environment.

Educational Status

The educational status of the populations of the sample households has been classified as illiterate, primary, middle, high, higher secondary and collegiate education.

Literate

According to 2001 census a literate is defined as a person who can both read and write with understanding in any language.

Illiterate

It is defined as a person who does not know how to read or write any language.

Occupation

The nature of work which the person has to perform is denoted by occupation.

Income

It refers to the wealth measured in money which has been at the disposal of an individual or a community per year of other unit to time. It may be considered to be a flow of purchasing power which may be expended at once on goods or services or retained for the purposes of capital accumulation.

Income is derived from various sources such as land, labour or capital. The word "Income" in this study refers to family monthly's income or earnings from various sources for the entire family.

Wages

The term 'wage' denotes all payments for labour services irrespective of the form or shape in which they are received such as daily basis, weekly basis, monthly basis and other payments in monetary or real terms (Stephen Pictchnis, G., 1975).

Expenditure

The term expenditure here is defined as family size expenditure and investment expenditure.

Public Sector

That part of the economy in which the state acts as entrepreneur.

Private Sector

That part of the economy which is left to private enterprise.

Status

Status is defined as the degree to which a person possesses characteristics valued in a particular society or has been discussed in terms of categories or kinds of persons.

Status of Women

At micro level the status of women is defined as a conjunction of the position she occupies as a student, worker, a wife and a mother.

Empowerment

It is a process giving employees more power to exercise control and take responsibility for their work. It gives more scope for individuals to exhibit their abilities by encouraging them to take decisions close to the point of impact. It is about encouraging both hands and minds of the people involved. It speeds up decision making process. It accelerates the response to time to meet the changing needs of the customer. It exhorts creativity of employees. It provides greater job satisfaction to them. Finally it leads to motivation, commitment and responsibility of the employees.

Organisation

An organisation maybe defined as a consciously co-ordinated social unit, composed of two or more people, that functions on a relatively continuous basis to achieve a common goal or a set of goals.

Work-family Conflict Variables

The concept of work-family conflict used in the present study is an extension and modification of Kopetman et.al., (1983) and used by E.D. Linda et.al. (1991) in their articles. In this extended model, (a) work involvement and work expectation are predictors of work conflict and work-family conflict, (b) family involvement and family expectation are predictors of family conflict and work-family conflict, (c) work conflict is a predictor of family conflict, (d) work conflict and family conflict are predictors of work-family conflict, (e) work conflict and work-family conflict affect an individual's quality of work life (QWL), (f) family conflict and work-family conflict affect an individual's quality of family life (QFL) and g) QWL and QFL jointly affect life satisfaction.

The definition of work-family conflict variables is given in the following paragraphs.

Work Involvement

The work involvement is defined as "a person's psychological response to his or her current work-role or job, the degree to which a person identifies psychologically with the job, and the importance of the job to the person's self-image and self concept" (Yoger, S. and Brett, J).

The work involvement is positively related to number of hours spent in the work. The hours spent in turn have been linked to increased work-conflict resulting from role overload (Staines, G. and et al., 1978).

Family Involvement

Family involvement is conceptualized as the 'degree to which a person identifies psychologically with family roles, the importance of the family to the person's self-image and self-concept, and the individual's commitment to family roles" (Yoger, S. and Brett, J.).

As work involvement, family involvement have also been shown to be positively related to the number of hours spent in family activities which in turn is to be linked to increased family conflict.

"Women's self-concept has traditionally been associated with their performance of the parenting and spouse roles" (Pleck, J., 1985). Sensitization theory predicts that when women are involved in the family role, it raises anxiety and guilt regarding their performance in non-traditional roles. Higher family involvement leads to more work-family conflict for women because they are playing a traditional family role along with a non-traditional role.

Work Expectations

Work expectations are defined as the pressure an individual perceives in assuming increased role responsibilities.

High work expectations have been significantly linked to high levels of work conflict (Greehnauns, J., and Beutell, N., 1985). Women do have mutually supportive and family roles. Central to the traditional roles of wife and mother is the obligation to be available to meet the needs of the family. Career women are unable to take time away from their family roles to satisfy work expectations. Several researchers have reported a positive association between work role expectations and work-family conflict. High work expectations have also been found to be positively associated with work-family conflict (Pleck, J., 1979).

Family Expectations

Family expectations are more in women employees. High family expectations have been linked to greater perception of family conflict (Bohen, H. and et al., 1981). Expectations surrounding the family role can evoke pressures that dominate the time of an individual. Family expectations are associated with the performance of the work role. Women have traditionally experienced stronger sanctions for non-compliance with family demands (Greehnauns, J. and Beutell, N.) Women's lack of control in balancing family needs against the demands of their job leads to greater work-family conflict.

Work Conflict

The work expectations cause work conflict since the women employees have to play two roles as mother and employee. The work-role characteristics such as the amount and scheduling of work time, that place demands and restrictions on an individual's work behaviour must be accommodated by women employees. These requirements contribute to work conflict. The conflict at work drains and pre-occupies the individual, making it difficult for her to participate adequately in family matters. The inaccessibility of the woman worker to a family member while she is working can create psychological problems in the family and lead to family conflict.

Family Conflict

The women are expected to manage their home domain, and such family responsibilities are likely to enter their work life. Since women have to take full responsibility for domestic work, the women's families are expected to make adjustments to accommodate the demands of her work-roles. Pleck (1977) claimed that there is an asymmetrical boundary between work and non-work and that for women, this boundary is permeable in the sense that non-work responsibilities are likely to enter and affect work life.

Work-Family Conflict

Work-family conflict occurs when an individual has to perform multiple roles: worker, spouse and in many cases, parent. Each of these roles imposes demands requiring time, energy and commitment. The cumulative demands of multiple roles can result in role strain of two types, namely overload and interference" (Kelly, R. and Voydanoof, P., 1985).

When the total demands of time and energy associated with the prescribed activity of multiple roles are too great for the roles to be performed adequately or comfortably, overload exists. Interference occurs when conflicting demands make it difficult to fulfil the requirements of multiple roles.

Women are more likely to allow the demands of the family role to intrude into the work role. This vulnerability of the female work role to family demands is a major source of work-family conflict because the sex role norm that women should take responsibility for the family, conflicts with the norms of the job role (Pleck, J., 1984).

Quality of Work Life

There is a link between the quality of work life and the levels of job satisfaction. Similarly work-family conflict is predicted to affect the quality of family life also.

Quality of work life is a comprehensive construct that includes an individual's job-related well-being to the extent to which work experiences are rewarding, fulfilling and devoid of stress and other negative personal consequences (Shamir, B. and Salomon, J., 1985).

Quality of Family Life

"Quality of family life is a construct that includes an individual's family-related well-being and the extent to which his or her roles as parent and spouse are rewarding, fulfilling and devoid of stress and other negative personal consequences" (Burke, R. and Weir, T., 1976). Family conflict has been negatively associated with quality of family life.

Life Satisfaction

"Life satisfaction is conceptualised as deriving from satisfaction experienced through having a good job and family life" (Sekaran, V., 1983). The women employees receive more life satisfaction from family on account of their traditional roles. Hence, the life satisfaction also influences the work-family conflict variables.

Chapter Scheme

The study is organized in seven chapters.

Chapter I introduces the subject, role of women, women work force and empowerment in the labour market, statement of the problem, objectives of the study, significance of the study, limitations, methodology, concepts and chapter scheme.

Chapter II reviews the earlier studies relating to women working in organized sector, and further the theoretical perspectives of women labour participation are discussed in this chapter.

Chapter III describes women work participation. Further the profile of the study area is also presented in this chapter.

Chapter IV analyses the characteristics of the sample women employees, the relationship between the characteristics of women employees and their familial characteristics and women workers' contribution towards family income.

Chapter V explains the work-family conflict, quality of work life and job satisfaction. Further it examines the inter-correlation among work-family conflict variables and assesses the contribution of independent variables to work-family conflict.

Chapter VI deals with women work participation and empowerment of women through decision making. The factors which influence the empowerment of women are also analysed.

Chapter VII presents the summary of findings along with conclusion and suggestions based on the study.

2

REVIEW OF LITERATURE AND THEORETICAL PERSPECTIVE OF WOMEN LABOUR PARTICIPATION

In a research, reviews are used to make the study more clear and comprehensive. This chapter contains two sections – one presents the review of literature and the other presents the theoretical perspective of women labour participation.

REVIEW OF LITERATURE

Status of Women

According to the study Levitan, Quinn and Staines (1971) full time working women in the united states are concentrated in jobs with lower pay and lower prestige than men. Women are paid less than men inspite of comparable work and qualifications. Women are paid low often, at a level below subsistence needs and few women of any class had expectations of anything letter.

Premilla Kapur in another study (1974) finds out the reasons for women's work. She says that women work not because of economic necessity but because they want to have economic independence, individual status or to have intellectual satisfaction to satisfy some of their sociological needs.

A study of Ritter and Hargans, (1975) examined data on 566 working women who identified themselves as 'middle class' in surveys conducted by the survey research centre. The results of their statistical analysis lend support to the view that the women's own occupational status, as well as that of their husbands, contributed to their self-identification as middle class.

Green field (1978) found that the results of a study proved the overall hypothesis that women in male-dominated jobs were significantly different from women working in female dominated jobs, in terms of family background feelings about being successful, and their attitude towards current jobs. Women in male-dominated jobs were more likely to be better educated and childless than were women in female-dominated jobs. Women in male dominated jobs were more likely to rate job-related success variables higher namely, achieving of very high salary and obtaining recognition from others on the job, etc, contrary to popular expectation that women in female-dominated jobs rate their current jobs as more important to them than do women in male-dominated and relatively balanced jobs.

In Sharaya Mhatre's study (1978) of women in banking a sample of 165 individuals from seven nationalised banks were drawn. The study has concluded that very few women are in senior position in banks and most of them are unmarried. The management has favoured women employees because they act as a check on union secretary and are tactful with clients.

O'Donnell and Anderson (1978) compared capable women from 10 traditional and 10 non-traditional fields to determine variables contributing to women's decisions to enter pioneering fields. The results showed that pioneers tended more often to have (1) mothers who graduated from college; (2) identified positive male influence on choice of college majors and career; (3) identified role-models; career goals; and role broadening work experience, and (4) parents who expected their daughters to work after graduation. Women in both traditional and non-traditional fields did equally well academically and neither of them preferred the conclusions drawn, that though no clear cut pattern of career choice influences emerged, women in pioneering fields appeared to have received more psychological support in formulation of their academic and career plans.

Karuna Ahmad (1979) in her work studied about the dominant trends in the employment of working women in India. The scope of this paper was to undertake a detailed treatment of the patterns of employment of educated women and analyse the degree of socio-economic independence enjoyed by them. The main finding of this study was that women of the upper and middle strata were traditionally denied access to education along with all other Indian women. Over the years, however, this situation is undergoing a slow and gradual change. One of the most noticeable trends in women's employment is that they tend to cluster in a few occupations like teaching, nursing and clerical related jobs. This clustering tendency has increased over the years. The tendency for women is to concentrate on a few limited employment opportunities open to women.

Studies by Nair and Mathew (1979) have shown how in order to avoid unionisation and payment of minimum wages and other benefits, the cashew industry is gradually moving units to the homes of women. Like coir industry the cashew industry is dependent on exploitation of cheap female labour. This is facilitated by putting into practice the system of piece rate wages so that the workers are paid much lower than what they would be paid otherwise in factories.

K.P. Singh (1979) in 'Status of Women and Population Growth in India', tried to find out the factors responsible for the rapid growth of population. The study supported the hypothesis that the higher the status of women the lower the fertility and vice versa. He feels that the social status of women is considered to be one of the factors that are related to fertility and population growth.

Lalitha Devi's (1982) "Status and Employment of Women in India" examined the role of white collar employment in contributing to higher status among women. The author explains that the employment has given women an opportunity to shoulder responsibility, play new roles, react with new people, face new situations etc. The effective performance of these new roles exploded the myth of female inferiority. They participate in socially meaningful and prestigious programmes.

Marine S.Shaul (1982) while making an international assessment on the states of women in local governments comments that there is no country in the world today where women have equal status with men in all of the major areas of life. Few women have held important positions but often, the women who have held national office are from upper class families with a history of political participation or are highly educated or single. In most developing countries, low level of education has led to women not being aware of their rights.

In Lalitha Devis' study (1982) of both employed and unemployed women it is believed that participation in the activities of voluntary organisation increases the status of women. Her study further showed that 23 per cent of the employed women played a very active role in their organisations while only 5 per cent of the unemployed took such an active role in the organisational activities.

The study conducted at the Centre for Development Studies (CDS) by Zachariah et.al (1994), focussed on the demographic changes in Kerala in the 1980's and their determinants. Three districts Ernakulam, Palakkadu and Malappuram were selected for the study. According to the authors, one of the most intriguing mortality differentials is with respect to work status of parents. Children of working mothers tend to have higher mortality rates than non-working mothers. The infant mortality rate for working and non working mothers are 54 and 29 respectively for the period 1980-89. The probable reason cited are: the shorter duration of breast feeding and the lesser amount of time the mother spends with the child. The joint effect of working status of the father and mother on infant and neo-natal mortality shows that infant mortality rates are higher among children where both father and mother are working. This may be due to the negative effect of mother's absence.

Krishnaji (1995) has analysed the impact of female work status on child survival with 1981 census data and found that in all the states working mothers experience a greater child loss than non-working mothers. He arrived at the conclusion that in India work among women can be closely identified with poverty and this identification of poverty of a lasting kind with working mothers results in a poor nutrition and health care among their children.

Role of Education

In a different study by Indira Devi (1987) to identify the changes emerging from education and employment of women in family, a sample size of 160 couples of Visakapattanam was taken. The major finding was that women's education and employment had helped to change the role performance, decision making and behaviour patterns, for egalitarian relations.

A study conducted by Manikyamba (1989) entitled, women in Panchayat Raj structure is an examination of the working of Panchayat Raj in general, the role of women as beneficiaries and benefactors in the socio-economic and political processes of development, and the assessment of the role of women presiding officers of the public relations. The sample of 88 women members covered the period from 1956 to 1989 and surveys their socio-economic background. The study revealed that education and participation in work were interrelated. Economic status gives a sense of confidence and encouragement to participate. Caste plays an important role in the selection of members. She was of the view that given the opportunity, talented and interested women could play very effective leadership role in politics.

Alagh N. Sharma and Seema Singh (1993) offer a detailed study of the issues relating to female migration in India. With education, the number of job-seekers among women tends to increase considerably and at a rate much faster than among their male counterparts.

Studies by the Tamil Nadu Muslim Graduates association over the last few years revealed that an increase of 10 per cent in the female literacy rate reduces the total fertility rate by less than half child per woman and about 2.3 children per woman with 80 per cent female literacy. The analysis of data for 15 major states covering 96 per cent of the country shows that female literacy and education are inversely related to the birth rates, death rates and infant mortality rates. Literacy in India means completion of the primary stage of education and therefore the anticipated results have not been achieved. Better results were seen in women who have completed at least the secondary education (Documentation on Women and Children, 1998).

Women Earnings and Their Contribution to the Family

Prabhai Rai (1975) has studied the Chicken Embroidery industry of Lucknow. It was estimated that about 45000 workers were engaged in chicken embroidery industry. About 97 per cent of the workers were women. The study also revealed that the women in this industry supplemented their family income by this work. A large number of them were deserted women and widows.

Singh (1980) reported that in a study of self-employed women in the settlement colonies of Delhi, a very small proportion of women was considered primary earners although 81 per cent of them stated that they worked to provide basic support to their families. The author points out the dependency assumption that a woman cannot be a primary earner as long as there is an adult male in the household. All household surveys underestimate the economic contribution of women to the household.

A survey conducted by Kumkumchadha (1981) in Neyyattinkara area show that around 65 per cent of the sample households were found to survive on female earnings. Interestingly while female earnings were the major sustaining force in these households women enjoyed powers of financial management and decision making (Documentation on Women and Children, 1998).

K. Rukmani (1981) studied about the women labour and employment in the cotton textile mills of Madurai district. Her important findings are as follows. Female workers are more illiterate (71 per cent). This is the reason for reduction in their employment opportunities and exploitations by employers of the mill workers are migratory in nature. The average working period is about 39 years and the model age group of women is between 41 to 50 years. And 61 per cent of the women workers like the job mainly on account of the attractive payment. The average monthly expenditure of women workers is Rs.490/-, the number of dependents per woman on an average was found to be 6. Woman worker's family saves monthly in the form of fixed deposit in their mills and 8 per cent of the women are provided with housing facilities by the employers. The most popular method of recruitment is through the relatives working in the mills.

Surinder Karur Sidhu, et al., (1986) have made a comparative study of the household expenditure pattern of families of working and non-working women in Ludhiana District of the Punjab state. The specific objective of this study is to find out the household expenditure pattern of the working women. The results obtained from the survey show that income was a dominant role in determining the consumption pattern of household. It was observed from the study that there were wide variations in the distribution of households among different income groups in the employed families. From the foregoing analysis one could conclude that expenditure pattern showed a high degree of association with the employment position of wives.

An exploratory research was conducted by Joshi (1988) to evaluate the impact of women's employment on work processes, organisational policies and practices. The apparent differences in work values of men and women were found out by 't'-test. It was observed that though women had longer years of work experience, they were earning less than men by doing non-technical jobs.

Desai and Jain (1994) in their study on rural south India noted that with the supposed conflict between children's need for care and mother's need for income, the role of domestic labour of women tend to be ignored. In addition to the domestic activities like cooking, cleaning etc. women spend considerable time making cow-dung cakes and collecting firewood etc which are rarely considered as economic activity. Although they are likely highly productive they are called "marginal economic activity" or "expenditure saving activity".

The study by A.V. Mohanasundaram (1995) showed that the urban informal sector like Tiruppur in Tamil Nadu where a large number of hoisery and khitting units have come up, has generated a significant amount of employment opportunities to household women who prefer to stay at home but are keen to earn for enhancing their family income. These women study in the home but undertake job work provided by the near by units. Further in industrially development areas such as Coimbatore city in Tamil Nadu, a large number of such avenues are available for this type of women.

Women Participation Rate

Ramachandran (1964) on the basis of a survey in Bombay found that a higher proportion of women who were in the labour force were non-collegiate and were from households where the head of the family was past middle age and where the per capita income was low. He further emphasised that the work participation rate of educated women was already low and more than 70 per cent of the educated women were non-workers in 1961. If the overall trend towards falling work participation rate of women continues the percentage of employed women from the educated sections could get still lower.

Kamala Nath (1970) examines the geographical differences in work participation ratio among women in different states and district. It is found in industry wise analysis of female-male ratio that women are represented in household sector of each industry and their number is small in modern organised sectors. Moreover, it is found that work participation of urban women is lower than that of rural women and that of literate women significantly lower than that of illiterate.

A study conducted by S.N. Ranade and Ramachandran (1970) to know the attitude of women towards part-time employment in Delhi and Bombay showed that more unmarried women than married are willing to take up the employment, especially as teachers and the reasons are mainly economic. It also showed that a large majority of women prefer to work in full time employment.

Patel and Dho Lakia (1978) examined the effect of certain development variables like income, marital status, child rearing, and caste on female participation rates and concluded that female participation rates tends to have a 'U'- shape curve with respect to income and that married women tend to have a higher participation rate than those not burdened with a family responsibility. Lastly socio-cultural factors have a significant bearing on the levels of female participation rate.

A study on the decline of women's participation in the workforce of the textile industry in Bombay by Mishra (1986) revealed that industrialisation has discriminated heavily against women. Decline of women workers occurred through a policy of not recruiting women employees. The main issue was not that of equal pay but of equal opportunities for employment.

Chandhury (1987) concluded that the increasing work participation of women had not been able to improve their lot and their share of developmental gains has remained much below what their contribution could justify. In the process of technological advancement, female workers have been displaced in many spheres. The energy and time consuming hard work coupled with calorie deficit in their food intake not oniy whittles down the working capacity of women but also heavily tells upon the upbringing of children and leads to increased child mortality. The study further revealed that the technology displacement of women labour on the one hand and lower wages rate to them on ground of productivity on the other, should be prevented through proper training to equip them to efficiently deal with developed techniques of production. There should be a proper estimate of the contribution of women work force to economic development in the domestic sphere as well as in the peasant farming in order to give them a larger degree of economic security and sense of self respect in the male dominated society.

According to the study of Malthier and Rogers (1987) in Britain, although female entry into some occupations such as the professions has been quite rapid, the over all employment distribution has only been marginally affected by these changes. Most women work in occupation that has been traditionally female dominated, and, as relatively few men have entered these occupations, sex inequalities in occupational distribution remains substantial.

Yoshie Ota (1999), President of Japan Institute of Workers Evolution has presented a paper on the title "Women in the Labour Force in Japan, Challenges and Opportunities for the New Millennium". She has highlighted the challenges faced by the working women of Japan 39.6 per cent of the total working population constitute female employees. A significant number of women choose not to participate in the work force. Almost 40 per cent of the female University graduates have never entered the job market. Even working women choose to take advantage of flexible and less demanding part-time jobs.

The paper of Muchlberger U. (2000) shows a theoretical connection between labour economics and sociology within an institutional approach, coupled with a gender order perspective and provides a useful framework for analysis. He concludes that the determinants of women's labour market behaviour are interrelated with a whole set of social and economic institutions which form a specific employment system.

By using the 1991 Census of Canada, Robert Carson and Peter Sheldon (2000) have estimated the labour market participation rates of female residents at Alberta. It was found that marital status was an insignificant determinant of labour market participation whereas the presence of children had a powerful influence on participation besides age, years of education and income of other members.

Angela (2001) has explained the factors influencing the labour force decisions either part time or full time. She has also studied the relationship between motherhood ideology and maternal labour force participation.

Working Condition

Based on 1969 working conditions, Cohen (1971) studied the wage differential between males and females working full time, full year and calculated an annual difference of $5000. Adjusting the differences in pay for the working age group between 22 and 64 for self-employed persons with unstable jobs and hours of work and also taking into account the fringe benefits, absenteeism, seniority, education and unionization, Cohen found these differences to be $2500 or 51 per cent of the original difference. He attributed this large difference to the concentration of women in lower paying jobs.

Mathew's (1979) study showed new women in coir industry worked for long hours and under insanitary and unhealthy conditions inorder to make reasonable returns. Indebtedness was endemic. Many suffered from diseases due to the work environment.

A study was undertaken (1986) by the department of historical studies in the Mother Theresa University in Kodaikanal. This study aims to find out the life style and working conditions of women. It has revealed a lot of interesting details. The women workers require a great deal of physical strength and energy. A critical account of the structural changes in the employment of women, presents the changing structure and rise in the working population. It was 175 million in 1971 and in 1981, it had increased to 220 million. There is a revolutionary character in the changing rate of growth of women employed.

A study in Latin America (1990) found that as more mid-wife women joined the work force, "accidents were arong the top five causes of death in women aged 50-59 in 11 out of the 18 countries surveyed". In five countries this was true for women over 65 as well. The women were mostly working in textile, footwear, food production, electronics and handicraft industries. Excessive heat, light and noise added to the hazards as well as exposure to toxic chemical and radiation.

Women Discrimination

According to Banerjee (1985) women's economic position was worsening because their role in the traditional economy slowly became redundant while their gains in the modern sector remained negligible. In a study about garment industry, it was found that home-based production system provided cheap labour to the industry. The natural skills of women were on sale at cheap rates in home-based work and the availability of large number of women contributed to the low wages among them.

Banerjee Nirmal's (1985) study of Bengal showed that women were pushed out by men when they needed jobs. Even in tea industry where women were considered essential, they lost their jobs in times of depression in favour of men. Computer technology has replaced the routine work of women.

Jeyalakshmi (1986) is of the opinion that the women's participation in the work force is deceptive as they under present the number of women actually engaged in productive work and underestimate the value of their work. Besides this, their economic contribution as labour at home is not recognized as it lacks monetary or market value.

According to the study of Hussain and Rukmani Rao (1988) on the state of women in public enterprises, it was found that there was stagnation in industry and women in general were delegated to low-skilled jobs. The management policies indicated that women did not require training or career planning. They were not considered suitable for supervisory jobs. Managers seemed to carry such stereotype impressions about women in society such as women are not interested in their work, and that they work to have fun and also that women are not and should not be ambitious.

According to the survey of the 46.58 per cent of women who reported facing harassment and discrimination at work, a majority said they faced mental harassment caused by acts such as writing, ogling, winking, passing of lewd remarks, reciting of obscene ballads or songs, abusing, lambasting and sexual gestures (Documentation on Women and Children, 1988).

A study by Mehta (1989) was to examine the extent of differences in employment and earning opportunities among similarly educated men and women. The study revealed that there exists inequalities in employment opportunities and earnings among men and women despite similar levels of education.

Shoma Chatterjee (1990) in the article entitled "Women in Management an uphill Task" has observed that in the patriarchal set up, all organisations in the private and public sector have been conditioned to accept only men in position of authority. But once women have entered the scene, the barriers are slowly breaking down by virtue of sheer grit, industry and their desire to prove their own worth in a male dominated world. Once the initial burden of proving their credibility and their commitment to the job has been established without doubt, the path is comparatively clear and the discrimination on grounds of being a woman begins to diminish visibly.

Nirmala Srinivasan and Janaki Raman (1991) in their study enquire into the problems of women employees. Not withstanding the adverse effects of gender bias, one is constrained to believe that misconceptions about women's career concepts also block their growth often. The assumption that women may not be interested in high profile jobs involving transfers, or excess working hours, results in reserving women for the conventional slots. Also when on account of childbearing and child-rearing activities women may not be always willing to accept increased responsibilities. These are often taken for granted as life-long involvements and in many situations stereo types inhibit the understanding of orientations, aspirations and visions of working women.

The study conducted by Bhanumathi Vasudevan (1992) covering all the Indian officers of the central government orgainsation threw up some rather disturbing findings, mainly that women were discriminated against in recruitment, advertising, in selection procedure, in work allocation, in career advancement and in personal ways, by other colleagues. Further, the findings revealsed discriminatory attitudes at all levels of staff from drivers to executives.

Nearly 50 per cent of working women surveyed in a recent study complained of gender discrimination and physical and mental harassment. The study (1997) carried out for the National Commission for Women (NCW) covered some 1200 women across India in the urban and rural areas and at various levels in the organised and unorganised sectors.

Dual Role

Kala Rani (1976) studied about educated married working women and discussed the dual role of working women. Most working women in her sample took up jobs to make use of their high or professional education which in turn afforded them a high standard of living. The study also attempts to find out the husband's attitude towards respondent's work. The study proves the hypothesis wrong that the working women's husbands do not help in household chores. The author suggested part-time employment for women that would suit a large number of housewives keen to fulfill professional interests and provide useful social contacts.

J.M. Unwalla's (1977) "A Study of Women Executives at Work and at Home" undertaken for her Ph.D in 1977 has probed into the phenomenon of the working women and listed its implications at work and house. She finds that women choose to work to prove themselves and attain social ascendancy. The study attempts to know the attitude of superiors towards working women. It shows that men in general accept a female boss just as well as they would a male boss.

Ramanamma (1979) in her study of graduate employed women in an urban setting investigated the problems faced by women at home and at work. It revealed that educated employed women brought about structural changes in the traditional institutions of family and marriage. The author feels that women who work outside have to face various situations, which are likely to generate conflicts. He has suggested part-time employment for women to utilise education and a provision of nurseries and crèches in the office to look after the young children of the employees.

Welch (1979) conducted a study on three groups of women: faculty wives with no outside employment; women in non-professional occupations; and those women in professional employment or occupation. The two working groups of women revealed less 'derived identity' than did the non-employed group of women and masculinity scores increased as a direct function of degree of departure from the housewife role. The conclusion drawn was that working wives (especially professionals) are more androgynous (high on both masculinity and femininity scales), than non-working wives.

There is a study carried out by Robert N. Kearney (1981) which focusses on the women in politics in Sri Lanka where she gives a historical background about the Sri Lankan women. She views that the traditional political role of women has been seen as originating in patterns of childhood socialisation that define women's role and concerns as limited to the private sphere at home and family, and that assigns the public sphere within which politics is located to men. From 1947 to 1977 only 4 per cent of the members of Sri Lanka's parliament have been women. She concludes that "However the opportunities for women to obtain political office, while meagre, do not appear to be markedly different from those of women in most other contemporary nation".

A sociological study of women in the police force has been done by Amarjit Mahajan (1982) who has concentrated his attention on the motivational factors behind women entering the police force. He has examined the problem from the historical perspective and has also paid attention to the role factor.

A study conducted by Hazel D' Lima (1983) titled "Women in Local Government in Maharashtra" deals with the role of women in local bodies namely Zillaparishad and Panchayat Samiti. The study traces the social emergence of women in the country, socio-economic, political background of women members in the Panchyat Samitis and Zillaparishads.

Radha Devi (1985) concluded that the burden of household duties might not always create a barrier to the employment of women. Women may participate in work outside home and would toil at home either because of their needs or the pressure from their husbands. What really matters in the context of increased work participation of women, is employment opportunities and not relief from household activities as such.

THEORETICAL PERSPECTIVE OF WOMEN LABOUR PARTICIPATION

The participation of women in the paid labour market is very different for men. Women's employment in both industrialised and third world countries is segregated both horizontally and vertically. Such segregation almost invariably corresponds to lower earnings and inferior working conditions for women and is accompanied by a division of labour within the home which accords women the major share of child care and other domestic responsibilities (Sinclair, 1991).

Orthodox Economic Theories

The marginal productivity theory could explain why women working equivalent number of hours per week in similar jobs earn less than men. To explain this phenomenon, it is necessary to show that women are less productive than men.

Monopsony Model

According to the micro economic theory of monopsony, the profit-maximising monopsonist, who faces an upward sloping supply curve of labour, hires labour upto the point where marginal labour cost equal marginal revenue product, pays workers a wage less than the value of marginal product.

In other words, a firm has greater monopsony power over women than over men (Peterfallon and Donald, 1988).

The Human Capital Model

Human capital theory assumes a direct causal relationship between education, productivity and wages. A large part of the explanation of lower wages may reside in lower productivity due to inferior preparation for work than to discrimination.

Prejudice Model

Prejudice models of discrimination are based on the notion that some employers indulge in their own sexual prejudices in making, hiring and other personnel decisions (Beeker, 1975-76).

Arrow tried to replace tastes for discrimination by beliefs (Arrow, 1972).

The Overcrowding Model

Overcrowding is defined as the interplay of a relatively low demand for a particular type of worker with a relatively large supply of that same type of worker. The first mention of this approach is found in Fawcett and Edgeworth (Chin Lee Gan, 1982).

Institutional Theories

Institutional economics explores how cultural institutions influence economic factors and, inturn, how they are shaped by those actors. Orthodox economics is noted for treating institutional factors as exogenous to markets. The attitudes, values and customs of society that orthodox economists accept as given, institutional economists seek to explore (Fischer, 1987).

Dual Labour Market Model

According to dual labour market theories (Kerr, 1954), there is a primary market consisting of primary jobs and there is a secondary market consisting of secondary jobs.

Certain workers become trapped in the secondary market owing to the institutional and sociological factors rather than the narrow (1976) economic variables. Barron and Norris suggest that the secondary labour market is essentially a female labour market, taking low earning levels as an indicator of the secondary status of a job.

Segmented Labour Market Models

Some workers have suggested the need to take into account more divisions than one of the primary and secondary and have characterised the labour market as 'segmented' rather than 'dualistic'. The model was first putforth by American writers (Edwards, Reich and Gordon, 1975).

Job Competition Model

Job competition model (Thurow, 1974), which challenges the human capital theory of wage determination is similar to the traditional theory of the labour market. Like the traditional theory, the job competition assumes a labour queue. But unlike the traditional theory, this theory argues that individuals compete for jobs on the basis of background characteristics and not on the basis of wages (Maya Shah, 1982).

Sex-Role Orientation Theories

Sex-role orientation or socialization theories focus on the problem of pre-labour market discrimination (Terborg and Illgen, 1975). Female socialization encourages, the acceptance of responsibility for domestic work and child care and discourages authoritativeness, aggressiveness quantitative or mechanical aptitude.

3

WOMEN WORK PARTICIPATION AND PROFILE OF THE STUDY AREA

This chapter deals with the women work participation rate in India, Tamil Nadu and Thoothukudi. Further it describes the profile of the study area.

WOMEN WORK PARTICIPATION

Women work participation rate in the country as a whole has been significantly lower than that of men. This has been depicted in Table 1.

Table 1
Work Participation Rates in India (1981-2001)

Year	*Category*	*Males (in per cent)*	*Females (in per cent)*	*Total*
1981	Total	52.6	19.7	36.7
	Rural	53.8	23.1	38.8
	Urban	49.1	8.3	30.0
1991	Total	51.6	22.7	37.7
	Rural	52.5	27.2	40.2
	Urban	49.0	9.7	30.4
2001	Total	51.9	25.7	39.2
	Rural	52.4	31.0	42.0
	Urban	50.9	11.6	32.2

Source: Censes of India, 2001 Provisional Population Totals, Paper 3, 2001.

Table 1 reveals that the total work participation rate has shown an increasing trend from 1981 onwards. It was 36.7 per cent in 1981, improved to 37.7 per cent in 1991 and further improved to 39.2 per

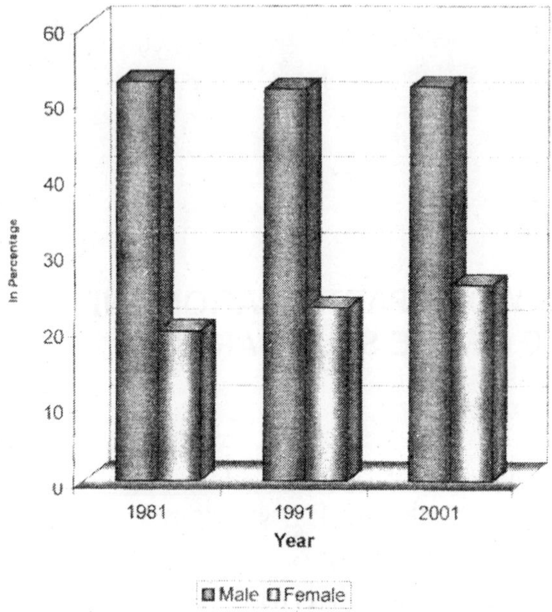

Figure 1: Total Work Participation Rates in India

cent in 2001. Increase in work participation rate is more perceptile in rural than in urban areas. Work participation rate in rural areas was 42.0 per cent and in urban areas was 32.2 in 2001. The work participation rate for females in rural areas has increased from 27.2 per cent in 1991 to 31.0 per cent in 2001 and in the case of urban areas, work participation rate increased from 9.7 per cent in 1991 to 11.6 per cent in 2001.

Women Work Force and Empowerment

The spread of education and the taking up of employment for economic independence has widened the outlook of women and they are gradually becoming aware of the importance of freedom and individuality. One tendency that is being observed is that the modern woman is gradually breaking through the shell of a narrow domestic existence and is beginning to participate in the larger life of the nation and even humanity. They have to be made aware of themselves and their tremendous skills and potentials due to the meaningful facilities of higher education, employment and high cost of living. More and more women are entering into the white-collared employment. In recent years, the employment trends project that the women in general are employed in lower echelons of administration and only in a few cases women are found to be occupying higher places. A large number of educated women mostly drawn from urban areas are now found to be enrolling themselves in employment exchanges for want of jobs. The level of unemployment among the educated women is increasing in the recent years. The highest motivation for work for a majority of Indian women is indeed the sheer economic necessity.

Table 2 reveals the total population and working population of India. The percentage of working population to total population was 46.75 in the year 1901. The percentage decreased to 39.2 in the year 2001.

Table 2
Working Population (1901 - 2001)

Year	*Total Population (in crores)*	*Total Working Population (in crores)*	*Col.3. as Per cent of Col.2*	*Total Female Working Population (in crores)*	*Col.5. as Per cent of Col.3.*
1901	28.83	11.14	46.75	3.73	33.48
1911	25.20	12.14	48.17	4.18	34.43
1921	25.12	11.79	46.93	4.01	34.01
1931	27.89	12.06	43.24	3.76	31.18
1941	31.85	12.92	40.57	3.94	30.50
1951	36.10	13.95	38.64	4.04	28.96
1961	43.91	18.86	42.95	5.96	31.60
1971	54.82	18.08	32.98	3.13	17.31
1981	68.52	18.05	26.34	3.21	17.78
1991	84.39	24.46	28.98	3.52	14.39
2001	102.52	40.25	39.20	4.95	25.70

Source: Census of India, 1991, Series I, (India) Paper 3 of 1991, Provisional *Population Tables*: Workers and Their Distribution.

The percentage of working population of women to total working population is 33.48. It was 28.96 in the year 1951 which increased to 14.39 percentage in the year 1991. But it increased to 25.7 in the year 2001. Analysis of data provided in the table helps to infer the percentage of women working. Population is declining gradually. However, the role of women employees is more important in public

Table 3
Literacy Rate in India

Year	*Male (in per cent)*	*Female (in per cent)*	*Total (in per cent)*
1951	18.3	8.9	27.2
1961	28.3	15.3	40.4
1971	34.5	22.0	46.0
1981	43.4	29.8	56.4
1991	52.1	39.4	63.9
2001	75.85	54.16	65.38

Source: Census of India, 2001 provisional population totals paper 3, 2001.

organisation with the growth of population, the women labour force has increased. In developing countries the female work participation rates are very low because of factors such as religion, tradition, cultural values, colonial ideology and evolution of social institutions. These causes are not excluded in India. According to 2001 Census, the female literacy rate was only 54.16 per cent.

Table 4 reveals that there has been a substantial fall in the share of agriculture in total employment from about 66.8 per cent in 1991 to about 56.7 per cent in 2001. The share of the secondary sector has improved from 12.7 per cent in 1991 to 17.5 per cent in 2001. Similarly there is a significant change in the share of the tertiary sector to about 25.8 per cent in 2001. According to 2001 Census of India, the data categorizing main plus marginal workers also indicate that agriculture accounts for 58.4 per cent of total workers. The secondary and tertiary sectors account for 41.6 per cent of total workers.

Table 5 reveals the total working population and work participation rate of India in 2001. It shows that out of a total population of 1025

Table 4
Sector-wise Employment in India 2001

(*in per cent*)

SL.No.	*Sector*	*1991*	*2001*
1.	Primary Sector	66.8	56.7
2.	Secondary Sector	12.7	17.5
3.	Tertiary Sector	20.5	25.8
	Total	100.0	100.0

Source: 1. Compiled from CMIE, Basic Statistics relating to the Indian Economy, Vol. I, All India, August 1993.
2. National Sample Survey Organisations.

Table 5
Sector-wise Workers in India 2001 and Work Particpation Rates

(in million)

Sector	*Population*			*Workers*			*Percentage of Workers*		
	Male	*Female*	*Total*	*Male*	*Female*	*Total*	*Male*	*Female*	*Total*
Rural	380.4	359.8	740.2	199.2	111.5	310.6	52.4	31.0	42.0
Urban	150.0	135.0	285.0	76.3	15.6	91:9	50.9	11.6	32.2
Total	530.4	494.8	1025.2	275.5	127.1	402.5	51.9	25.7	39.2

Source: Registrar General of India.

million, 402.5 million were workers, of these 275.5 million were males and 127.0 million females. Out of a total rural population of 740.2 million, workers accounted for 310.6 million, with 199.2 million being males and 111.5 million being females. In the urban population, out of a total of 285.0 million, 91.9 million persons constituted the urban workforce. Among them, 76.3 million were males and 15.6 million were females. But the percentage of women working population to total working population was 14.39 in 1991 but it increased to 25.7 per cent in 2001.

Analysis of data provided in Table 5 helps to infer that the percentage of women working population is increasing gradually. However, the role of women employees is more important in public organisation with the growth of population, and the increase in the women labour force. In developing countries female work participation rates are very low because of factors such as religion, tradition, cultural values, colonical ideology and evolution of social institutions. These factors are quite typical of India

Empowerment implies a state of mind and attitude of a person. Women in their historical journey, were forced to naturalise and internalise male domination resulting in their marginalisation from the mainstream life.

In the last two decades women have been demanding a legitamate autonomy in all matters that have a bearing on their empowerment. An empowered woman has a positive self image and takes an active part in decision making related to herself, her family and outside. Empowerment emerges in the form of an awareness in the women.

"By empowerment" women face challenges boldly and overcome barriers in their life through which they increase their ability to shape their own lives and environment.

A nation's march onwards progress and prosperity will remain a dream, its aspirations unfulfilled and unrealised, till women actively participate in the development process.

Women in India are not able to contribute their best to the development of the society. It is because women are in backwardness in the field of education and social, economic and political spheres. The high incidence of illiteracy among women constitutes one of the greatest barriers to their development. It limits their scope for development. NCW reported in 1988, that the female workforce operates within highly exploited conditions characterised by long hours of work, low earnings, lack of security, lack of support and safeguards at the organisational level.

The role of women can be summed up in 4 M's – March, Mother, Manager and Mover.

The reasons for women not joining the main stream of development include, lack of recognition of women's special needs for education, training, technology, communication and access to resources, lack of information about women's role, castes, etc. All these stand as obstructions in integrating women into the mainstream programmes.

All over the world women have been victims of oppression and male domination. This leads to powerlessness and it prevents them access to public resources, legal redress and ability to fight for their rights.

The Beijing Bonanza of 1995 is a powerful agenda for the empowerment of women. "Women need crutches nor handouts. They need to be empowered to take their rightful place on an equal footing with men. They need to be liberated from discrimination and exploitation. If they are not shackled and suppressed in a deliberate manner, women are capable of making greater contribution to the country in the next 50 years than they have been habituated to during the past 50 years" stated the first lady of India Ms. Usha Narayanan.

"The urgent agenda for womanhood in India and the platform of action for unfoldment of the female personality demands radicalisation of the ethos of society and the corpus jurist of the country" said the eminent jurist, Mr. Justice V.R. Krishna Iyer, on the occasion of the celebration of the International Women's Day on 8, March 1998. An all pronged, multifaceted battle must be launched against the injustice being heaped on women. The need of the hour is equal participation of women in governance and in the decision making process. It was observed that women are the better persons of the world who respected the human rights of men. Men should learn from women folk how to respect the human rights of the other gender.

The means of empowerment are:

1. Education
2. Health and Nutrition
3. Economic independence
4. Legal awareness
5. Organisational support and
6. Intervention programmes.

Women represent half of the human capital of the nation and they should be given all chances of equal representation in all fields. (N. Jeyabalan, 2001).

Experts on women's issues have said that the publication of the document was linked to the declaration of 2001 as the year of empowerment of women. This is a positive step indeed in the first year of the 21st century. Incidentally, the Ninth five year plan which is nearing an end, has also focused on women's issues. Its objective is to involve women as important agents of social change and development (1997-2002). For the first time, Empowerment of women has been made an objective. Further, women's development issue has been elevated to the level of a macro objective, under the plan.

Empowerment is the key factor for making women agents of social change and development. Therefore, women cease to be instruments of development and they become its principal catalysts. The ninth plan focussed on both women specific and women - related sectors and chalked out strategies accordingly.

For instance it laid emphasis on creating environment for women to exercise their rights both within and outside home and providing adequate representation of women in decision making for reserving one third of seats in parliament and state legislatures for them (Anju Grover, 2002).

Women Work Participation in Urban Area

Majorities of the urban women workers of developing countries are employed in the informal sector. There is high concentration of women in occupations characterized by low skill requirement, low productivity, low income, less stability, and less security. Half of the women are in the urban informal sectors and home based workers.

According to the 2001 Census, the urban female work participation was 11.6 per cent. This was higher than the previous years' percentage. Women's work within the household sector is always neglected while formulating their real workload. The ratio of the urban female workers is even less than one third of their male counterparts during the last three decades of the census enumeration. Although there is an increase and progress in the working women's percentage from 1971-2001, the increase was very marginal. In 1991 the total women labour force was 22.27 per cent. Out of it, 16.03 per cent women were categorised as main workers and 6.24 per cent as marginal workers between 1981 and 2001 both in rural and urban areas. Marginal workers' participation increased only in rural areas, but remained unchanged in urban areas.

Table 6
Women Work Participation Rates in Urban Area

Year	*Category*	*Female (in percentage)*
1971	Urban	7.2
1981	Urban	8.3
1991	Urban	9.7
2001	Urban	11.6

Source: Censes of India, 2001, Provisional Population Totals Paper 3, 2001.

The modern organisations can reap maximum benefits by having proper gender mix. Women employees, though equal, are different. They exhibit different kinds of talent through their creative thinking interpersonal skills innovativeness and hard work. An interesting phenomenon in Indian workforce is that women employees are more at lower level positions and much less at middle level (that is) reaching about 10 per cent of the total workforce. The number is a mere one per cent at top level. As such the organisations are deprived of the services of accomplished women managers. The reason behind this is that while women at lower hierarchical levels are shown sympathy and given some amenities, as they climb the managerial ladder, the male managers fail to recognise them as their equals. The top management should realise that what the women employees need most is not sympathy but an identity and recognition. Because sympathy makes them feel weak. Many career women would like to balance their quota of work between office and home. They can forgo neither of them. Children and domestic responsibilities are facts of a woman's life and they should be accepted as such. They never cease to exist in her life. To extract fullest potential from a woman employee perks like creches, transport should be provided to them to facilitate the smooth performance of these extra responsibilities. These perks should be provided as they are provided to any male employees, than as a special favour to the women employees.

Even the women's mindset and attitudes have to be changed. Not many women even today come forward to take up challenging positions. They prefer routine and comfortable life even at the cost of their career advancement. They prefer to stay at the same place even without promotions. Attitudinal changes have to be inculcated at a very early stage to change such a mindset. Such education should be provided to them that teach self-confidence, self-esteem, independence and development of personality. Empowerment of women takes place only when she is independent in all spheres of her life.

Organised Sector

The organised sector usually refers to employment in the public sector and in private sector establishment employing 10 or more persons. It is commonly believed that wages in the organised sector are much higher than in the unorganised sector. Moreover, the organised sector being regulated also provides greater job security and other benefits. Jobs in the public sector receive much higher wages and accompanying benefits than those in the private sector for similar skills. Besides this, the public sector offers greater job security. Employment in the organised sector crept up slowly from 27.37 million in 1994 to 28.22 million in 1999-2000. This was largely the consequence of virtual stagnation of employment in the public sector during 1994-2000. But the private sector employment grew from 7.93

million in 1994 to 8.70 million in 1999-2000. But since the public sector accounted for over 69 per cent of total employment in the organised sector, private sector employment was not able to effectively offset the declaration experienced in the public sector employment (Ruddar Datt and K.P.M. Sundaram, 2003).

Employment in the organised sector has been hardly 8.34 per cent, of which the public sector accounts for 5.77 per cent and private sector only for 2.57 per cent in the total employment generated during 1999-2000. The organised sector is dominated by the public sector which accounts for 70 per cent of the total employment in this sector. This is mainly in the areas of (i) mining, (ii) electricity and water and (iii) community and social services. These three collectively constitute nearly 60 per cent of the public sector employment figures and unfortunately, all of them show negative employment elasticity. This only underlines the fact that the public sector contributed to a very small extent in total employment generation during 1993-94 to 1999-2000 (Ruddar Datt and K.P.M. Sundaram, 2003).

Table 7 shows that the total number of workers employed in the public sector in 1971 was 71 lakhs, but by March 2001 their number grew to about 191 lakhs. Since employment in the public sector was confined to the organised sector, public sector employs 70 per cent of the workers employed in organised sector.

Table 7
Public and Private Sector Employment in India

(in lakhs)

Year	*Public Sector (1)*	*Private Sector (2)*	*Total (3)*	*(1) as Percentage of (3) (4)*
1971	71	121	192	55
1981	155	74	229	68
1991	190	77	267	71
2001	191	87	278	70

Source: Compiled from Economic Survey, 2002-2003.

The public sector is entrusted with the responsibility of developing heavy and basic industries, social and economic infrastructure while the private sector is broadly given the right to develop consumer goods industries. While banks and financial institutions, railways, civil

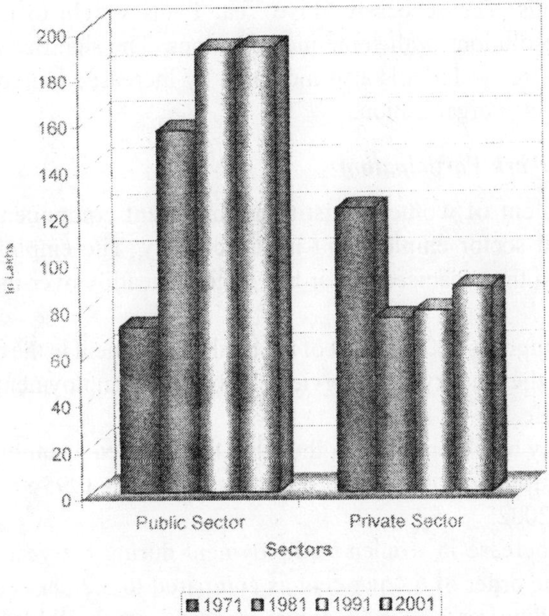

Figure 2: Public and Private Sector Employment in India

aviation, power generation and distribution etc., are in the public sector, the private sector in India embraces the whole of agriculture and allied activities, plantations, mining, internal trade both retail and wholesale etc. However the most organised private sector is the corporate industrial sector.

Women Employment in the Organised Sector

Employment in the organised sector requires certain minimum qualifications and most of the educated women employees are drawn from middle and upper classes. Very few women from the lower classes are found. Working for an equal number of hours along with their counterparts in addition to family responsibilities puts a greater strain on them.

The public sector is based on the basic concepts of public ownership. The benefits accruing through profit have to percolate to the general public in an equitable manner. The employees have no special claims other than those in similar jobs in other government institutions. The successive Five Year Plans sought to implement policy resolutions with some modifications. The significance of the public sector in India is also indicated by increased employment in public sector organisation.

Women Work Participation

Employment of women constitutes important components of the organised sector employment in the country. The employment of women in the organised sector has gone unsteadily over the last ten years.

It comprises 16.3 per cent of the total employment in the organised sector in the country. An overview of women's employment is given in the table.

It may be observed from the table that women's employment in the organised sector went up from 45.27 lakh in 1995-96 to 50.48 lakhs in 2002.

An increase in women's employment during the year 2001-02 was of the order of 6.4 per cent as compared to 5.2 per cent during the preceding years 1995-96. It may be seen from the Table 8 that the share of women's employment to total employment in the organised sector has risen steadily from 16.3 per cent 1995-96 to 18.6 per cent in 2001-2002.

Table 8
Employment of Women in the Organised Sector of India

Year Ended 31st March	*Women Employment (in lakh)*	*Percentage Change over Previous Year*	*Total Employment (in lakh)*	*Percentage of Women Employment to Total Employment*
1987	33.40	2.2	253.88	13.2
1988	34.36	2.9	257.12	13.4
1989	35.45	3.2	258.97	13.7
1990	36.46	2.8	263.53	13.8
1990	37.81	3.7	267.33	14.1
1992	39.08	3.4	270.56	14.4
1993	40.26	3.0	271.77	14.8
1994	41.54	3.2	273.75	15.2
1995	43.04	3.6	279.87	15.4
1996	45.27	5.2	277.80	16.3
2002	50.48	6.4	271.47	18.6

Source: Compiled from Economic Survey, 2002-2003.

Work has been defined in 1991 Census as "participation in any economically productive activity". Such participation may be physical or mental in nature work and involves not only actual work but also effective supervision and direction of work. It also includes unpaid work on farm or in family enterprise. The tracheotomy of main worker, marginal worker and non-worker was introduced in 1981 Census and was continued in 2001 Census.

A person is considered a main worker if he had worked for the major part of the year (that is) six months (183 days) and more. If he had not worked for the major part of the year (that is) had he worked for less than six months or less than 183 days he was treated as a marginal worker. Persons, who had not participated in any economic activity even for a day during the year preceding the day of enumeration, were considered non-workers.

The table shows that the main workers account for 77.8 per cent and marginal workers account for 22.2 per cent. The proportion of males among main workers was 87.3 per cent and that of female workers, 57.2 per cent. Among the marginal worker the males represent 12.7 per cent and females 42.8 per cent. This implies that females account for a much larger proportion as marginal workers–nearly 43 per cent. In rural areas, the proportion of main and marginal workers among female work force was 54 per cent and 46 per cent respectively, but in urban areas, this proportion was 79 per cent and 21 per cent respectively.

Table 9
Main and Marginal Workers in India (2001)

(*in million*)

Sector	*Main*			*Marginal*		
	Male	*Female*	*Total*	*Male*	*Female*	*Total*
Rural	85.0	54.1	74.0	15.0	45.9	26.0
Urban	93.4	78.8	91.0	6.6	21.2	9.0
Total	87.3	57.2	77.8	12.7	42.8	22.2

Source: Registrar General of India.

Out of the total marginal workers in rural areas, 37 per cent were males and 63 per cent females. It shows that gender distribution of marginal workers in rural areas was fitted towards females. As against this, out of the total marginal workers in urban areas, 60.2 per cent were males and 39.8 per cent females. The share of females in urban gender distribution of workers was relatively higher as compared with that of rural areas.

The growth of the organised sector in our country has been sluggish throughout the plan period. It barely accounts for one tenth of the total workers employed in the organised sector that includes establishment in public sector from non-agriculture, establishments in private sector employing ten or more workers. A bulk of employment in the organised sector comes from the public sector. The number of workers employed in organised sector has increased from 26.82 per cent in 1991 to 27.15 per cent in 2001.

In India, women account for a small share of the industrial labour force. As far as female participation in organised sector in India is concerned women constituted 18.6 per cent of the total workers in organised sector. Their participation in many industries such as jute, mines, textiles is declining steadily. In many industries as modern capital intensive technology is introduced, women lose out because men preferred to tend the new machines. Technological changes and mechanization have been displacing women because vocational guidance and training in new skills for girls have been neglected.

Women Work Participation in Tamil Nadu

Women in Tamil Nadu in the recent past have emerged as potentially significant contributors to the country's growing labour force. According to 2001 Census, women accounted for 48 per cent of the total population in the country. Of this Tamil Nadu accounted for 6.22 per cent. The proportion of women in total workers had increased from 30 per cent in 1991 to 34.7 per cent in 2001. With regard to work participation rate for women (41.33 per cent), the state occupied the fifth place among the States as on 2001.

Turning to the organised sector employment, the proportion of women in total employment had improved from 21.2 per cent in 1991 to 36.81 per cent in 2001. The share of women had further gone up to 28 per cent in the total organised sector employment during 2001. Committed to the cause of the development of women, the State Government had set apart 30 per cent of the 'Service intake' to women aspirants. Under special employment generation schemes also 40 per cent was earmarked for women.

Going by the industry-wise classification, 'community, social and personal services' under the public sector and 'manufacturing' under the private sector attracted a major share of women employees (more than 80 per cent and 60 per cent respectively).

According to 2001 Census the female work participation rate of the State was 18.42 per cent against 13.10 per cent in 1991 Census. At the all India level the work participation rate was slightly higher at 37.59 per cent in 2001 against 34.7 per cent in 1991.

Table 10
Work Participation Rate in Tamil Nadu – 2001

(*in Per cent*)

Sector	*Persons*	*1991*	*2001*
Rural	Male	58.28	59.38
	Female	38.50	41.33
	Persons	48.49	50.39
Urban	Male	52.78	56.37
	Female	13.10	18.42
	Persons	33.34	37.59

Source: Census of India, 2001.

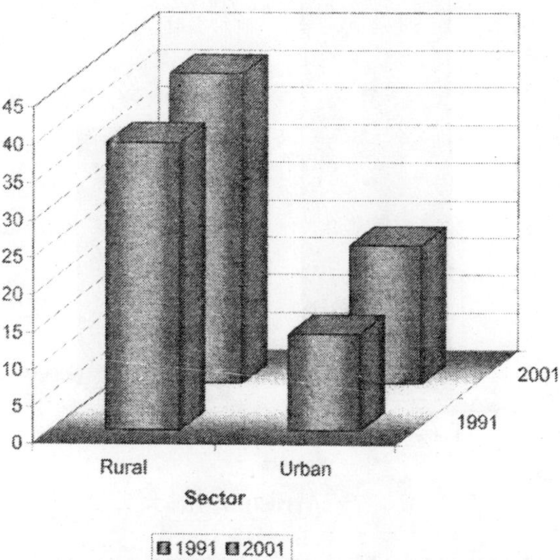

Figure 3: Women Work Participation Rate in Tamil Nadu (in Percentage)

Table 11
Employment Level of Organised Sector in Tamil Nadu – 2001

(in Per cent)

Sector	*Persons*	*1991*	*2001*
Public Sector	Male	12.57	11.57
	Female	3.23	4.20
	Total	16.00	15.77
Private Sector	Male	5.31	5.46
	Female	1.79	2.98
	Total	7.10	8.44

Source: Directorate of Employment and Training, Madras-5.

The above table shows that women's employment level in both public and private sectors in Tamil Nadu has improved in 2001 though the share of total employment in public sector has declined from 16 per cent in 1991 to 15.77 per cent in 2001.

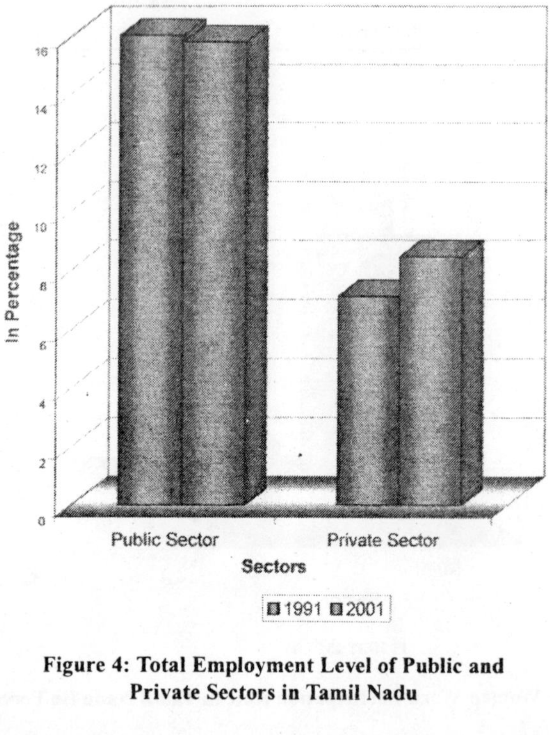

Figure 4: Total Employment Level of Public and Private Sectors in Tamil Nadu

Table 12
Percentage of Working Population to Total Population in Tamil Nadu – 2001

Population	*Total Workers*	*Main Workers*	*Marginal Workers*	*Non-workers*
Male	18153275 (58.06)	16346879 (52.28)	1806396 (5.78)	13115379 (41.94)
Female	9658372 (31.32)	7337732 (23.79)	2320640 (7.53)	21183813 (68.68)
Persons	27811647 (44.78)	23684611 (38.13)	4127036 (6.65)	34299192 (55.22)

Source: Census of Tamil Nadu, 2001.

From the above table, it is very clear that the percentage of female marginal workers was higher than the male marginal workers. And also it is clear that women work participation in Tamil Nadu had slightly increased in 2001. The proportion of main workers to the total population has come down from 41.29 per cent in 1991 to 38.13 per cent in 2001. But the proportion of marginal workers has risen to 6.65 per cent in 2001 from 2.84 per cent in 1991. The ratio of main workers and marginal workers in India to total population is 36.43 per cent and 4.34 per cent respectively. Thus Tamil Nadu's working population is comparatively higher than all India average except marginal workers. There is a marginal improvement in percentage of female main workers to total population also.

According to 2001 Census, the female literacy rate in Tamil Nadu was 64.55 per cent. It has been increased from 51.33 per cent in 1991.

Table 13
Literacy Rates in Tamil Nadu

(*in Per cent*)

Year	*Male*	*Female*	*Total*
1991	73.75	51.33	62.66
2001	82.33	64.55	73.43

Source: Census of Tamil Nadu, 2001.

The table shows the total workers and non-workers in Tamil Nadu. It shows that Tamil Nadu has 96,58,372 female workers which is 34.73 per cent of total workers. Also it has 2,36,84,611 main workers which is 85.16 per cent and 41,27,036 marginal workers which is

Table 14
Tamil Nadu at a Glance (2001)

Sl.No.	General Details	Tamil Nadu	Percentage to Total Population
1.	Area (sq.km.)	130058	
2.	Population:	62110839	
	(a) Male Population	31268654	50.34
	(b) Female Population	30842185	49.66
	Rural Population	34869286	56.14
	Urban Population	27241553	43.86
3.	Total Workers	27811647	44.78
	(a) Male workers	18153275	58.06
	(b) Female workers	9658372	31.32
	Rural Workers	17572083	28.29
	Urban Workers	10239564	16.49
	(a) Main workers	23684611	38.12
	(b) Marginal workers	4127036	6.65
	(c) Other workers	12573697	45.21
4.	Non-workers	34299192	55.22

Source: Census of Tamil Nadu, 2001.

14.84 per cent of total workers in Tamil Nadu. Also 3,42,99,192 non-workers constitute 55.22 per cent of the total population.

Pattern of Women Employment

The employment of women in public and private sectors as on 31st December 2001 and percentage of state figures to national figures are presented in Table 15.

It may be observed from the table that out of 50.48 lakh women employees in the organised sector at the end of December 31, 2001,

Table 15
Women Employment in Public and Private Sectors - 2001

Sector	Employment (in lakhs)		Percentage of State Figures to National Figures
	India	Tamil Nadu	
Public	28.96	4.20	14.5
Private	21.52	2.98	13.8
Total	50.48	7.18	14.2

Source: Census of Tamil Nadu, 2001.

28.96 lakh were in the public sector and the remaining 21.5 lakh in the private sector in India. Also out of 7.18 lakh women employees in the organised sector 4.2 lakh were in the public sector and the remaining 2.98 lakh were in the private sector. In Tamil Nadu women's employment in both public and private sectors registered a growth of 14.5 per cent and 13.8 per cent respectively during the year 2001.

Women Work Participation in Thoothukudi District

Thoothukudi is a special grade municipal town and head quarters of a newly formed district. The district could be termed as industrially advanced with a majority of the industry located in and around Thoothukudi. There are large numbers of private coconut oil mills within the town. The public sector undertakings are the Thoothukudi Thermal Power Station unit, Heavy Water Plant and Port Trust.

The total population of this district as per 2001 Census is more than 15 lakhs. The density of population per square kilo metre is 315 as against the 428 for the state. The sex ratio is 1050 females for every 1000 males. The percentage of literacy is 81.5 per cent. The district has a schedule caste population of 2,88,954, which is around 18.4 per cent of the total population.

The following table explains the general details of Thoothukudi district. According to 2001 Census the total population of Thoothukudi district was 15,72,273. Of this 7,66,823 are males and

Table 16

General Details of Thoothukudi District - 2001

Sl.No.	*General Details*	*District*	*Urban*
1.	Area in hectares	416650.66	21706.22
2.	Residential Houses	42343	59872
3.	Households	382260	157647
4.	Population		
	Males	766823	327569
	Females	805450	337204
	Total	1572273	664773
5.	Children (0-6) years		
	Male	94431	39535
	Female	89980	38188
	Total	184411	77723

Source: National Information Centre, Thoothukudi.

8,05,450 females. Out of this, 5,93,868 males and 5,37,538 females are literates. Thoothukudi district has 42,343 residential houses and 3,82,260 households. In the age group of 0-6 years, the male children are 94,431 and female children are 89,980.

The table reveals that female literacy was 75.64 per cent in 2001. It has increased from 64.57 in 1991.

Table 17
Literacy Rates in Thoothukudi District

(*in Per cent*)

Year	*Male*	*Female*	*Total*
1991	82.02	64.57	73.02
2001	88.66	75.64	81.96

Source: National Information Centre, Thoothukudi.

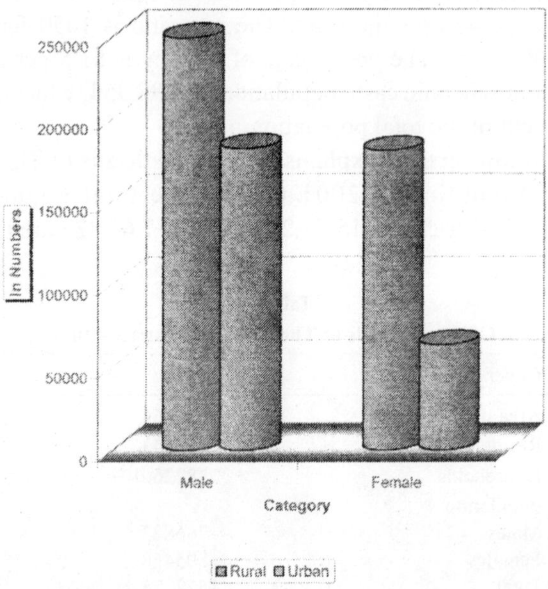

Figure 5: Total Workers in Thoothukudi District – 2001

The table shows that the female marginal workers are more in number in both rural and urban sectors than males. But the female main workers are more in rural sector than in urban sector.

Table 18
Total Workers and Non-workers in Thoothukudi District – 2001

Sector		*Population*	*Total Workers (Main + Marginal)*	*Main Workers*	*Marginal Workers*	*Non-Workers*
Rural	Male	437599	248691	221286	27405	188908
	Female	466212	180192	136056	44136	286020
	Total	903811	428883	357342	71541	474928
Urban	Male	326488	181695	174224	7471	144793
	Female	335444	63104	53172	9932	272340
	Total	661932	244799	227396	17403	417133
Total	Male	764087	430386	395510	34876	333701
	Female	801656	243296	189228	54068	558360
	Total	1565743	673682	584738	88944	892061

Source: National Information Centre, Thoothukudi.

The given Table 19 shows 31984 employees are working in Thoothukudi district. Of this 17,342 are male employees and 14,642 are female employees. Among them the state government employees are 66.83 per cent, and local body employees 5.84 per cent and aided

Table 19
Number of Employees by Service, Type and Sex in Thoothukudi District

SL.No.	*Service Type*	*Total Number of Employees*			
		Male	*Female*	*Total*	*Percentage*
1.	Regular	14939	7575	22514	70.39
2.	Temporary	447	221	668	2.09
3.	Fixed pay	187	67	254	0.79
4.	Consolidated pay	367	739	1106	3.46
5.	Contingent staff (full-time)	80	40	120	0.38
6.	Contingent (part-time)	43	72	115	0.36
7.	Fixed MR Noon-meal & Village ESTT	1132	5351	6483	20.27
8.	Daily Wages	51	5	56	0.18
9.	Sec. Workers on Daily Wages	3	3	6	0.02
10.	Work charged employees	36	2	38	0.12
11.	Honorarium	55	566	621	1.94
	Eligible for Bringing into Regular ESTT				
12.	Without relaxation of rules	1	0	1	0
13.	By Relaxation of rules (5 & 6)	1	1	2	0
	Total	17342	14642	31984	100

Source: National Informatics Census, Thoothukudi.
Primary Census Abstract, 2001.

schools and colleges 24.40 per cent. Of this, the regular employees are 70.39 per cent and fixed MR Noon-meal and Village ESTT are 20.27 per cent which is shown in the table. From this, it is clear that female employees under consolidated pay and also fixed MR Noon-meal and Village ESTT are more in number.

In Table 20 shows the number of employees in Thoothukudi district. It has been found out that number of employees were high in the State Government offices (20,882) where the female workers were accounted for 9,601. This has been followed by the female employees in aided schools (4,171), aided colleges (272) and local bodies (268) in the study area.

Table 20

Number of Employees in Thoothukudi District

SL.No.	*Service Type*	*Total Number of Employees*			
		Male	*Female*	*Total*	*Percentage*
1.	Regular	14939	7575	22514	70.39
1.	State Government Offices	11281	9601	20882	65.29
2.	State Public Undertakings	454	38	492	1.54
3.	Local Bodies (Panchayat Union)	262	140	402	1.26
4.	Local Bodies (Town Panchayat)	397	49	446	1.39
5.	Local Bodies (Village Panchayat)	250	20	270	0.84
6.	Local Bodies T.S. under M.Act	18	17	35	0.11
7.	Local Bodies T.S. under P.Act	0	0	0	0
8.	Local Bodies Municipalities	850	268	1118	3.5
9.	Local Bodies Corporations	0	0	0	0
10.	Marketing Committees	0	0	0	0
11.	Universities	201	28	229	0.72
12.	Judiciary	219	32	251	0.78
13.	Autonomous Bodies	0	0	0	0
14.	Aided Schools	2724	4171	6895	21.56
15.	Aided Colleges	635	272	907	2.84
16.	Other Agencies	51	6	57	0.18
	Total	17342	14642	31984	100.00

Source: National Informatics Census, Thoothukudi. Primary Census Abstract, 2001.

Thus, it is inferred that majority of women workers participate in the State Government offices in Thoothukudi district.

The given Table 21 shows female main workers of Thoothukudi urban town under industrial categories. Women workers in manufacturing and processing category form 17.85 per cent. Transport and communication contribute 5.6 per cent, while trade and commerce have 11.54 per cent. Construction workers amount to 4.95 per cent and other services are 48.78 per cent.

Table 21

Percentage of Female Main Workers Under Industrial Categories in Thoothudukudi - 2001

SL.No.	*Main Workers*	*Thoothukudi Town Percentage of Women Worker*	*Tamil Nadu Percentage*
1.	Cultivators	8 (0.11)	24.84
2.	Agricultural Labourers	13 (0.19)	34.64
3.	Livestock, Forest & Fisk	35 (0.50)	2.03
4.	Mining & Quarry	4 (0.06)	0.30
5.	Household Industries (Hhi)	732 (10.42)	3.52
6.	Manufacturing & Processing Others	1254 (17.85)	10.51
7.	Construction Workers	348 (4.95)	2.15
8.	Trade & Commerce	811 (11.54)	8.68
9.	Transport & Communication	394 (5.60)	3.09
10.	Other Services	3428 (48.78)	10.24
	Total	7027 (100)	100.00

Source: National Information Centre, Thoothukudi.

From this, it is very clear that the women main workers are more in other services than the above industrial units.

PROFILE OF THE STUDY AREA

This section provides a glimpse of the physical features, agro-elimatic conditions, demographic features and infra structural set up of the Thoothukudi district.

Thoothukudi District-Historical and Cultural Background

Thoothukudi was ruled over by the Pandya kings before the British rule. During the freedom struggle, it was the birth place of many brave patriots. The darkness of British slavery was dispelled by the selfless sacrifice of these devoted patriots. Veerapandia Kattapomman with his undaunted fighting spirit, Bharathiar with his fiery, rich poems of patriotism and V.O. Chidambaranar who floated the Swedishi ship against the British, fought the foreign rule. They made the soil of Thoothukudi proud and rich in cultural heritage.

District at a Glance

Thoothukudi 'the pearl city of India' is the newly formed district by bifurcating the original Tirunelveli district into Tirunelveli district (western portion) and Thoothukudi district (eastern portion).

"The Government of Tamil Nadu in their G.O. Ms.No.535/ Revenue Department dated 23.04.1986 have ordered the formation of a new district viz.. Thoothukudi district. Thoothukudi district was inaugurated on 19.10.1986 by the chief minister of Tamil Nadu and started functioning as the 20th district with effect from 20.10.1986 with the headquarters at Tuticorin". But in 1997, it was changed as the district of Thoothukudi, with Thoothukudi as its centre.

The District covers an extent of 4,621 sq.km in the South-Eastern portion of Tamilnadu and it is rectangular in shape. It is bounded by Virudhunagar and Ramanathapuram district in the North, Kanyakumari district in the South, Gulf of mannar in the east and Tirunelveli district in the west. The district is roughly triangular in shape between 8°-05' and 9° - 80° of the northern latitude and 77°-05' and 78°-25' of eastern longitude.

Physical Features

There are no high mountains in the district Red Mounds or small hills are found in Tiruchendhur, Srivaikundam, Sathaankulam and

THOOTHUKUDI DISTRICT

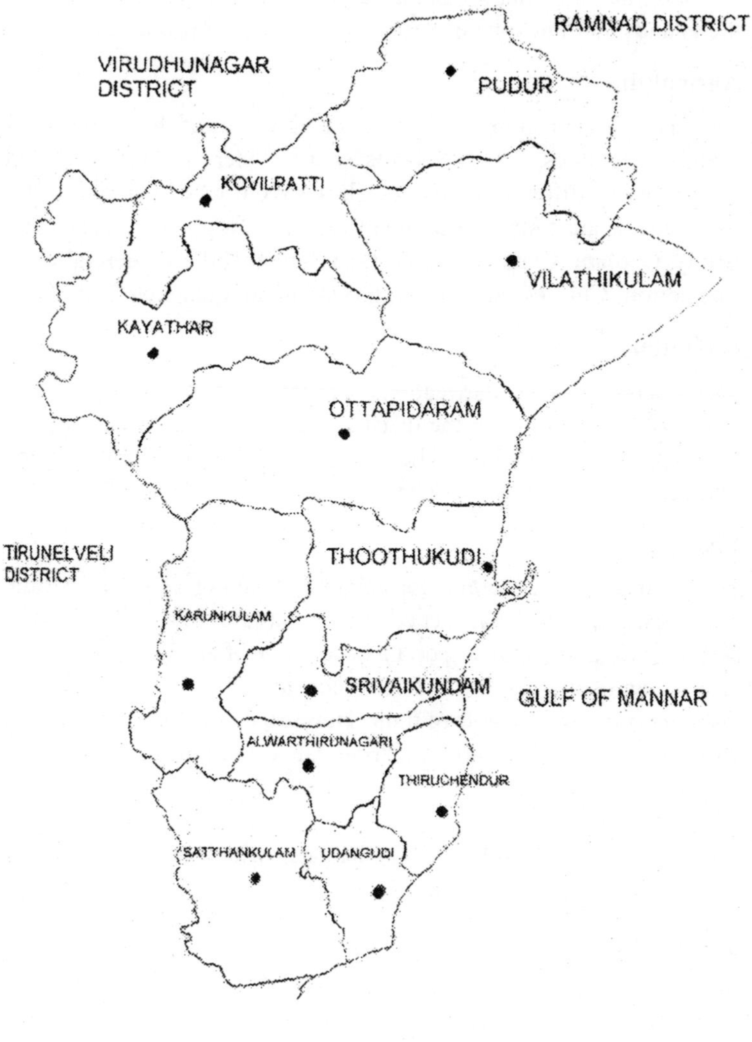

Vijayaramarpuram. The stretch of land that tilts to the east in Srivaikundam is made fertile by the Thamiraparani river. This river flows through Punnaikayal and joins the Bay of Bengal, Malattar, Mambiaru, Vaippar and Manimuthaar.

Mineral Resources

Gypsum, Ilammanide, Monazide, Hyduim, Limestones, Corals from the Islands and Phosphate are some of its natural resources.

Agriculture

The main food crop in the district is paddy. Out of the total area of 4,50,954 hectares, 2,11,811 hectares have been brought under the cultivation of different crops, which work out to 47 per cent of the total area of the district. The important food crops in the district are paddy, Cholam, Cumbu, ragi, Varagu, Samai and commercial crops like cotton, Chillies, Sugarcane, groundnut and banana.

Irrigation

The different sources of irrigation are channels, lanks and wells which corer 45,159 hectares in the district. Out of the total area irrigated, well irrigation covers 17,709 hectares, tank irrigation 22,538 hectares and channel irrigation 4,876 hectares for the year 1991-92.

Fisheries

This district is an important coastal district having a vast coastal line of 160km and territorial water covering thousands of hectares. Fishing next to agriculture, is an important occupation of the district. Tuticorin is a major fishing centre. It is also considered to be the only pearl fishing centre in the whole of India. Besides, it is also noted for chunk fishing. Nearly 35000 MT of marine fish are produced per annum.

Forestry

The area under forestry is 12724 hectares which occupies 2.77 per cent of the geographical area.

Population

The population of the district as per 2001 Census was 15,72,273, of which 7,66,823 were males and 8,05,450 females. The population density in the district is 315 per sq.kms against the state average of 428 per sq.kms. The percentage of scheduled caste population is 18.4 and that of scheduled tribe population is 0.2 per cent of total population. The percentage of urban population is 42.28 and that of rural population is 57.72 of the total population. The literacy percentage of male is 88.3 and female is 75.1. Total literacy percentage of this district is 81.5.

Table 22
Urban Population in 2001 Census

	Females	*Males*	*Total*
India	13,52,19,060	15,01,35,894	28,53,54,954
Tamil Nadu	1,36,14,583	1,38,69,415	2,74,83,998
Thoothukudi District	3,37,204	3,27,569	8,05,450

Source: National Informatic Centre, Thoothukudi

From this table it is clear that the total urban population of India is 28,53,54,954 of this, female population is 13,52,19,060. In Tamil Nadu female population is 1,36,14,583. Out of the total population of Tamilnadu, Thoothukudi district's urban population is 8,05,450. Among this the female population is 3,37,204. From the table we can say that female urban population in Thoothukudi district is more in number than male population.

The given table shows the literacy level in urban areas.

Table 23
Literates According to 2001 Census

		Person	*Male*	*Female*
Tamil Nadu	Total	4,05,24,545	2,28,09,662	1,77,14,883
	Rural	2,03,19,498	1,18,35,689	84,83,809
	Urban	2,02,05,047	10,9,73,973	92,31,074
Thoothukudi	Total	11,31,406	5,93,868	5,37,538
	Rural	6,22,745	3,29,518	2,93,227
	Urban	5,08,861	2,64,350	2,44,311

Source: National Informatic Centre, Thoothukudi

From this table it is obviously clear that urban female literacy is 45.69 per cent of the total population of the urban literates in Tamil Nadu. At the same time the total urban literates in Thoothukudi district is 2.52 per cent of the total population in Tamilnadu. Of this, the female literacy is 1.21 per cent.. From this table, it is also very clear that female literacy level in Thoothukudi is lower than male literacy.

The following table shows the urban working population

Table 24
Urban Workers to Total Population - 2001 Census

(*in Per cent*)

Area	*Females*	*Males*	*Persons*
India	11.60	50.90	32.20
Tamil Nadu	18.42	56.37	37.59
Thoothukudi District	4.01	11.56	15.57

Source: National Informatic Centre, Thoothukudi

From the table, it is clear that the total urban workers to total population in India is 32.20 per cent. Of this 11.60 per cent are females. Out of 37.59 per cent of the workers in Tamil Nadu, 18.42 per cent are females. In Thoothukudi district 4.01 per cent are female urban workers, out of 15.57 of the urban workers.

From this table it is clear that the percentage of female urban workers in Thoothukudi district is very low. This is because of lack of employment opportunities for women.

Women Work Participation in Thoothukudi District

The given table shows the classification of female workers in Thoothukudi district. According to 2001 Census, workers were classified into main workers, marginal workers and non-workers. Out of the total main workers 5,84,738 female main workers are 1,89,228 and male main workers are 3,95,510. Out of 88,944 marginal workers,

Table 25
Number of Female Workers in Thoothukudi District - 2001

SL.No	*Workers Details*	*Persons*
1.	Main workers	
	Male	3,95,510
	Female	1,89,228
	Total	5,84,738
2.	Marginal workers	
	Male	34,876
	Female	54,068
	Total	88,944
3.	Non workers	
	Male	3,33,701
	Female	5,58,360
	Total	8,92,061

female workers are 54,068 and male workers are 34,876. Out of 8,92,061 non-workers, females are 5,58,360 and males are 3,33,701.

Table 26
Number of Employees by Social Group Sex in Thoothukudi District

SL.No.	*Social Group*	*Male*	*Female*	*Total*	*Percentage*
1	Other communities	2521	1350	3871	12.10
2	B.C	10257	9832	20089	62.81
3	M.B.C	1840	1393	3233	10.11
4	S.C	2583	1983	4565	14.27
5	S.T	141	85	226	0.71
Total	17342	14642	31984	100.00	

Source: National Informatics Centre Thoothukudi: Primary Census Abstract in 2001.

The number of employees by social group and sex in Thoothukudi district is shown in the above table. From this table, we can say that BC group of people are more in Thoothukudi district and also female employees under BC social group is greater than the other social group.

Industries

The district constitutes 70 per cent of the total salt production of the State and meets 30 per cent requirement of our country. There are two industrial estates one at Kovilpatti with 11 units and the other at Thoothukudi with 20 units. The former is managed by SIDCO and the latter by SIPCOT. Small scale industries such as match industries, food-based and metal based industries are generally concentrated in Kovilpatti and Thoothukudi taluks. There are 2200 and above small scale industries registered in the district and about 12 major industries. These are engaged in the production of cotton and stable yarn, caustic soda, PVC resin, fertilizers, soda ash, carbon dioxide gas in liquid form, etc. The important major industries are SPIC, TAC, Dharangadhara Chemical Works, Loyal Textiles Ltd., Madura Coats Ltd., Sterlite Copper Industries, Kilburn Chemicals, Ramesh Flowers, Nila Sea Foods, Deva and Co. and Transworld Granite Industries.

The public sector undertakings are the Thoothukudi Thermal Power Station Unit, Heavy Water Plant (HWP) and Port Trust. The District Industries Centre and the Tamil Nadu Industrial Investment

Corporation are catering to the needs of the small and large scale industries.

The Government is also encouraging unemployed youth and others to start industries by providing financial assistance and technical guidance.

Topography

The river Tambirabarani flows through this district. The area under the river basin within the district is 78,698.8 hectares. According to topography, the district can be divided into three regions. The northern part consists of black soil, mostly dependent on seasonal rainfall for agriculture; the central part is irrigated by water flow from the Western Ghats; and the southern part is red loam area. The normal rainfall is 662.mm. which is less than the state normal of 1009.1mm.

Administration

It has two divisions, eight subdivisions and 468 villages. At the local bodies level, Thoothukudi has two municipalities, 12 Panchayat unions, 20 town panchayats 408 village panchayats and 10,121 small villages and eight taluks, one Parliament Constituency and seven assembly constituencies. It has three revenue divisions and eight revenue sub-divisions.

Educational Institutions

Thoothukudi has one Maritime Academy, two B.Ed Colleges, 10 Arts Colleges, one Medical College, six Polytechnic Colleges, one Agricultural College, one Fisheries College, eight I.T.I Schools, 97 Higher Secondary Schools, 73 High Schools, 284 Middle Schools, 1076 Primary Schools and many education oriented courses.

Health Department

Thoothukudi has 19 Government hospitals, one Medical College hospital and 249 health welfare departments.

Public Welfare Department

For the benefit of the public, there are 164 banks. To maintain law and order there are 44 police stations. Of this, there are two women police stations remaining under the direct control of superintendent of police and 62 Theatres for entertainment.

Transport and Communication

The district has a road length of 2310km, comprising of 1232 km of metallic roads, 665 kms. of non-metallic roads and 413 km of kutcha roads.

The district is served by 413 post offices covering 3270 persons per post office. There are 61 telegraphic offices in the district which serve an average population of 22,140 per office. Similarly, there is one radio set for every 31 persons in the district.

Welfare Schemes for Women

Many government schemes like Tamilnadu village women's development programme is implemented successfully. Under this scheme, women at the age group of 21-60 coming below the poverty line are organised in self-helping groups with 12 to 20 members each. The government, bank and non-government institutions help these women to rise in socio-economic levels and education.

By giving sound exercise to these self-help groups an awareness and opportunity is being created for them.

Weekly savings schemes among the groups enable the members belonging to the same, to procure loans at a low interest, thus protecting them from exploiting money-lenders.

The government through several schemes provide opportunities to increase the financial position of the people. Through nationalised banks and other government organizations like Indira Mahila Goshi, loans for lesser interest are given. The women are able to do business and thus increase their income.

To rise in literacy and to be educated, the right coaching is given to these rural women. As much they are able to free themselves from social evils and get equal rights.

To be freed from social tyranny, to be economically stable, to have the light of literacy, to rise in cultural behaviour and to enjoy health, these self-help organisations try to strengthen themselves. In this district, 612 self-service organisations operate successfully under this rural women welfare scheme.

4

CHARACTERISTICS OF THE SAMPLE RESPONDENTS AND THEIR FAMILIAL PROFILE

Today, economic independence is considered to be the prime basis for improving the status of women in India. It is generally agreed that women's participation in work would result in reducing their dependency, enhancing their social and economic activities, as well as empowering them to assert more in the household decisions. In India, women cannot be viewed as a homogenous group as the society is stratified on the basis of class, caste and religion. It has been observed that participation in work especially for females remains tied to class, caste and religious affiliations. In order to grasp the nature of these causal relationships, it is imperative to understand the socio economic characteristics of women work participants. This chapter attempts to analyse the objectives namely,

1. Studying the relation between personal characteristics of women work participants and their familial characteristics.
2. Examining the variation in income between public and private sector women employees and assess the women workers contribution towards family income.

For this, the analysis of the present chapter has been classified under the heads namely,

(i) Socio-economic characteristics of the sample women work participants.

(ii) Family characteristics of the respondents

(iii) Relationship between family characteristics and income of the respondents

(iv) Variation in monthly income between different groups of women workers and

(v) Women workers' contribution towards family income.

SOCIO-ECONOMIC CHARACTERISTICS OF WOMEN WORKERS

This section attempts to describe the socio-economic characteristics of the sample women respondents.

Table 1 presents the distribution of the sample women respondents according to their age.

Table 1
Age Wise Classification of The Sample Respondents

Age	*Public*			*Private*		
(Years)	*Central*	*State*	*Total*	*Industry*	*Service*	*Total*
Below 30	11 (17.19)	29 (29.30)	40 (24.54)	7 (8.86)	6 (10.34)	13 (9.49)
30-40	33 (51.56)	42 (42.42)	75 (46.01)	36 (45.01)	31 (53.45)	67 (48.90)
40-50	16 (25.00)	21 (21.21)	37 (22.70)	27 (34.18)	16 (27.59)	43 (31.39)
50 and above	4 (6.25)	7 (7.07)	11 (6.75)	9 (11.39)	5 (8.62)	14 (10.22)
Total	64 (100)	99 (100)	163 (100)	79 (100)	58 (100)	137 (100)

Source: Survey Data.
Note: Figures in parentheses are percentage to the total.

Age wise classification of the sample respondents is furnished in Table 1. It is observed that out of 64 respondents working in central government, 11 (17.19 per cent) of them fall under the age group of below 30, 33 (51.56 per cent) of them fall under the age group of 30-40, 16 (25.00 per cent) of them and four (6.25 per cent) of them fall under the age groups of 40-50 and 50 and above respectively. Further it shows that out of 99 state government respondents, 29 (29.30) of them and 42 (42.42) of them fall under the age groups of below 30 and 30-40 respectively, 21 (21.21 per cent) of them and seven

(707 per cent) of them fall under the age groups of 40-50 and 50 and above respectively. In public sector, out of 163 respondents, 40 (24.54 per cent) of them fall under the age group of below 30 and 75 (46.01 per cent) of them, 37 (22.70 per cent) of them and 11 (6.75 per cent) of them fall under the age groups of 30-40, 40-50 and 50 and above respectively.

It is also observed from the Table 1 that the age wise classification of the respondents working in private sector, out of 79 respondents in industry, seven (8.86 per cent) of them fall under the age group of below 30, 36 (45.57 per cent) of them fall under the age group of 30-40, 27 (34.18 per cent) of them and in (11.39) of them fall under the age groups of 40-50 and 50 and above respectively. It is also inferred that out of 58 respondents in service sectors, six (10.34 per cent) of them and 31 (53.45 per cent) of them fall under the age groups of below 30 and 30-40 respectively, 16 (27.59 per cent) of the and five (8.62 per cent) of them fall under then age groups of 40-50 and 50 and above respectively. Further it shows that out of 137 private sectors, 13 (9.49 per cent of them fall under the age group of below 30, 67 (48.90 per cent) of them, 43 (31.39 per cent) of them, 14 (10.22 per cent) of them fall under the age groups of 30-40, 40-50 and 50 and above respectively.

Thus it is inferred from the analysis that more than 45 per cent of the respondents belong to the age group of 30-40 years in both sectors in the study area.

Table 2 shows the educational status of the women workers in public and private sectors.

Table 2 points out that out of 64 respondents working in the central government sector, 10 (15.63) of them have technical qualifications like bachelor's degree or diploma in engineering. 12 (18.75 per cent) of them are post-graduates. 36 (56.25 per cent) of them and six (9.38 per cent) of them possess graduate degree and S.S.L.C/ PUC level education respectively. Out of 99 respondents working in state government sector, 58 (58.59 per cent) of them are graduates, 26 (26.26 per cent) of them are post graduates and 8 (8.08 per cent) 7 (7.07) of them possess S.S.L.C/PUC and technical qualification respectively. It is also observed that in public sector, out of 163 respondents 94 (57.67 per cent) of them and 36 (23.31 per cent) of them possess graduate and post graduate qualification respectively

Table 2
Educational Qualification of The Sample Respondents

Qualification	*Public*			*Private*		
	Central	*State*	*Total*	*Industry*	*Service*	*Total*
S.S.L.C/PUC	6 (9.36)	8 (8.08)	14 (8.59)	27 (34.18)	36 (62.07)	63 (45.99)
Graduates	36 (56.25)	58 (58.59)	94 (57.67)	36 (45.57)	12 (20.69)	48 (35.04)
Post graduates	12 (18.75)	26 (26.26)	38 (23.31)	11 (13.92)	6 (10.34)	17 (12.41)
Technical	10 (15.63)	7 (7.07)	17 (10.43)	5 (6.33)	4 (6.90)	9 (6.57)
Total	64 (100)	99 (100)	163 (100)	79 (100)	58 (100)	137 (100)

Source: Survey Data.
Note: Figures in parentheses are percentage to the total.

and 17 (10.43) of them and 14 (8.59 per cent) of them have technical and S.S.L.C./PUC qualification respectively.

It is also inferred from Table 2 that regarding the educational qualification of the respondents working in private sector, out of 79 respondents working in private industrial sector, 5 (6.33 per cent) of them have technical qualifications, 11 (13.92 per cent) of them have post graduate degree. 27 (34.16 per cent) of them and 36 (45.57 per cent) of them have S.S.L.C/PUC and graduate qualification respectively. Out of 58 respondents working in service sector of private sector, 36 (62.07 per cent) of them have S.S.L.C/PUC, 12 (20.69 per cent) of them have graduate and 6 (10.34 per cent) and (6.90 per cent) of them possess post graduate and technical qualification respectively. It is also clearly indicated that in the private sector, out of 137 respondents 63 (45.99 per cent) of them and 48 (35.04 per cent) of them possess S.S.L.C/PUC and graduate qualification respectively. 17 (12.41 per cent) and 9 (6.57 per cent) of them have post graduate and technical qualifications respectively.

Thus it is inferred from the analysis that all the sample women respondents are well educated and more than 90 per cent of them are graduates, post-graduates and possess technical qualifications.

The respondents are classified on the basis of their marital status in Table 3.

Table 3
Classification of The Respondents on The Basis of Marital Status

Marital Status	*Public*			*Private*		
	Central	*State*	*Total*	*Industry*	*Service*	*Total*
Married	59 (92.19)	88 (88.89)	147 (90.18)	72 (91.14)	54 (93.10)	126 (91.97)
Unmarried	3 (4.68)	6 (6.06)	9 (5.52)	3 (3.80)	2 (3.45)	5 (3.65)
Widow/Divorce	2 (3.13)	5 (5.05)	7 (4.29)	4 (5.06)	2 (3.45)	6 (4.38)
Total	64 (100)	99 (100)	163 (100)	79 (100)	58 (100)	137 (100)

Source: Survey Data.
Note: Figures in parentheses are percentage to the total.

Table 3 reveals that out of 64 respondents working in central government, 59 (92.19 per cent) of them are married, three (4.68 per cent) of them are unmarried and two (3.13 per cent) of them are widows/divorcees. Out of 99 sample respondents working in state government, 88 (88.89 per cent) of them are married, six (6.06 per cent) of them are unmarried and 5 (5.05 per cent) of them are widows/ divorcees. It is also deduced from the Table 3 that with regard to the marital status of the public sector, out of 163 respondents, 147 (90.18 per cent) of them are married, 9 (5.52 per cent) of them are unmarried and 7 (4.29 per cent) of them are widows and divorcees.

Further, it is derived from the Table 3 that regarding the martial status of the respondents working in private sector, out of 79 respondents working in private industrial sector, 72 (91.4 per cent) of them are married, 4 (5.06 per cent) of them are widows and divorcees and 3 (3.80 per cent) of them are unmarried. Out of 58 respondents working in service sector, 54 (93.10 per cent) of them are married, 2 (3.45 per cent) and 2 (3.45 per cent) of them are unmarried and widows/divorcees respectively.

It is clearly observed from the Table 3 that, in the private sector, out of 137 respondents, 126 (91.97 per cent) of them are married, 6 (4.38 per cent) and 5 (3.65 per cent) of them are widows/divorcees, and unmarried respectively.

Thus it is deduced from the table that 98 percent of the public sector workers are married and 84 per cent of the private sector respondents are married.

The distribution of the sample respondents based on the reasons for taking up employment is presented in Table 4.

Table 4
Reasons for The Employment of The Respondents

Reasons	*Public*			*Private*		
	Central	*State*	*Total*	*Industry*	*Service*	*Total*
To increase the family income	32 (50.0)	48 (48.48)	80 (49.08)	44 (55.70)	30 (51.72)	74 (54.01)
Self satisfaction	8 (12.5)	10 (10.10)	18 (11.04)	12 (15.19)	8 (13.79)	20 (14.60)
To make use of education	14 (21.88)	31 (31.31)	45 (27.61)	8 (10.13)	5 (8.62)	13 (9.49)
To have a status	5 (7.81)	6 (6.06)	11 (6.75)	6 (7.59)	6 (10.34)	12 (8.76)
Personal security	3 (4.69)	2 (2.02)	5 (3.07)	5 (6.33)	4 (6.50)	9 (6.57)
Others	2 (3.13)	2 (2.02)	4 (2.45)	4 (5.06)	5 (8.62)	9 (6.57)
Total	64 (100)	99 (100)	163 (100)	79 (100)	58 (100)	137 (100)

Source: Survey Data.
Note: Figures in parentheses are percentage to the total.

It is found from Table 4 that in the public sector, both central and state, among the various reasons for taking up work, to increase the family income accounted for 49.08 per cent followed by the reason to make use of education which is accounted for by 27.61 per cent. The other reasons were the self satisfaction (11.04 per cent), to have a status (6.75 per cent) personal security (3.07 per cent) and others (2.45 per cent).

In the case of private sector, out of 137 respondents, 74 (54.01 per cent)of them have the reason to increase the family income. It is followed by ‘self satisfaction (14.60 per cent), ‘to make use of education’ (9.49 per cent) and to have a status’ (8.76 per cent). The same trend was found in industry and service group also in the study area.

The monthly income of the respondents has been classified into three groups as shown in Table 5.

The results of Table 5 reveal that out of 64 respondents working in public central government sector, 44(68.75 per cent) of them are

Table 5

Classification of Monthly Income of The Respondents

Monthly Income (in Rs.)	*Public*			*Private*		
	Central	*State*	*Total*	*Industry*	*Service*	*Total*
Below 5000	8 (12.5)	7 (7.07)	15 (9.20)	9 (11.39)	8 (13.79)	17 (12.41)
5000-10000	44 (68.75)	78 (78.79)	122 (74.85)	60 (75.95)	47 (81.04)	102 (74.45)
10000 and above	12 (18.75)	14 (14.14)	26 (15.95)	10 (12.66)	3 (5.12)	18 (13.14)
Total	64 (100)	99 (100)	163 (100)	79 (100)	58 (100)	137 (100)

Source: Survey Data.

Figures in brackets denote percentages to total.

coming under the middle income category. 12 (18.75 per cent) of them are coming in the second category viz., above middle income group. 8 (12.5 per cent) of them come under below 5000. They lead a hand-to-mouth living. Out of 99 respondents working in state government, 78 (78.79 per cent) of them come under the category of 5000-10,000. 14 (14.14) and 7 (7.07) of them are in the next category viz., 10,000 and above and below 5000 respectively.

It is inferred from Table 4 that out of 163 respondents of public sector 122 (74.85 per cent) of them come under the monthly income category of 5000-10,000. 26 (15.95 per cent) and 15 (9.20 per cent) of them come under the monthly income category of 10000 and above and below 5000.

It is also observed from the Table 4 that out of 79 respondents of the private industrial sector workers, 60 (75.95 per cent) of them come under the monthly income group of 5000-10,000. 10 (12.66) and 9 (11.39 per cent) of them come under the second and third category income group of 10,000 and above and below 5000.

It is noticed from the Table 4 that the out of 58 respondents work in private service sector, 3 (5.17 per cent) of them come under the monthly income category of Rs.10000 and above. 8 (13.79 per cent) of them are private service sector workers whose income is below Rs.5000. 81 per cent of the workers (47) belong to the monthly income category of Rs.5000-10000.

Out of 137 respondents working in private sector 102 (74.45 per cent), 18 (13.14 per cent) and 17 (12.41 per cent) of them come under the income group of Rs.5000-10000, Rs.10000 and above and below Rs.5000 respectively.

FAMILY CHARACTERISTICS OF THE RESPONDENTS

Family is a social institution, formed by marriage and it serves a number of purposes. It is an organized system of relationships and norms. It provides security, love, affection and all kinds of emotional and social support like needs fulfillment. Hence, family background forms the base for women's work participation and in this section, an attempt has been made to discuss the family characteristics like religion, caste, family size, type of family, spouses' income and family income.

The distribution of women respondents by religion is given in Table 6.

Table 6
Religon Wise Classification of The Respondents

Religion	*Public*			*Private*		
	Central	*State*	*Total*	*Industry*	*Service*	*Total*
Hindu	43	83	126	55	48	103
	(67.19)	(83.84)	(77.30)	(69.62)	(82.76)	(75.18)
Muslim	5	4	9	6	2	8
	(7.81)	(4.04)	(5.52)	(7.59)	(3.45)	(5.84)
Christian	16	12	28	18	8	26
	(25)	(12.12)	(47.18)	(22.79)	(13.79)	(18.98)
Total	64	99	163	79	58	137
	(100)	(100)	(100)	(100)	(100)	(100)

Source: Survey Data.
Figures in brackets denote percentages to total.

Table 6 clearly exhibits that out of 64 respondents working in central government 43 (67.19 per cent) belong to Hinduism, 16 (25 per cent) belong to Christianity and only 5 (7.81 per cent) of them are Muslims. It is further understood that out of 99 respondents working in the state government, 83 (83.84 per cent) of them belong to Hinduism, 12 (12.12 per cent) belong to Christianity and only 4 (4.04 per cent) are Muslims.

Out of 163 respondents working in public sector, 126 (77.30) of them 28 (17.18) of them and 9 (5.52 per cent) of them are Hindus, Christians and Muslims respectively.

It is also clearly indicated that out of 79 respondents working in private industrial sector workers, 55 (69.62 per cent) of them are Hindus, 18 (22.79 per cent) of them are Christians and 6 (7.59 per cent) of them are Muslims. It is further observed that out of 58 respondents working in private service sector, 48 (82.76 per cent) of them belong to Hinduism, 8 (13.79 per cent) of them belong to Christianity and only 2 (3.45 per cent) of them are Muslims.

Out of 137 respondents working in private sector, 103 (75.18 per cent), 26 (18.98 per cent) and 8 (5.84 per cent) of them are Hindus, Christians and Muslims respectively.

Caste wise classification of the sample respondents is given in Table 7.

Table 7
Caste Wise Classification of The Respondents

Caste	*Public*			*Private*		
	Central	*State*	*Total*	*Industry*	*Service*	*Total*
OC	46 (71.88)	81 (81.82)	127 (77.91)	61 (77.22)	47 (81.03)	108 (78.83)
BC/MBC	10 (15.62)	12 (12.12)	22 (13.50)	13 (16.46)	7 (12.07)	20 (14.60)
SC/ST	8 (12.50)	6 (6.06)	14 (8.59)	5 (6.32)	4 (6.90)	9 (6.57)
Total	64 (100)	99 (100)	163 (100)	79 (100)	58 (100)	137 (100)

Source: Survey Data.
Figures in brackets denote percentages to total.

From the Table 7, it is clearly indicated that out of 64 caste wise classifications of the sample respondents working in public central government, 46(71.88 per cent) of them belong to other caste (OC), 10 (15.62 per cent) of them belong to backward and most backward classes (BC/MBC) and 8 (12.50 per cent) of them belong to schedule caste and schedule tribes (SC/ST). Further, it is derived from the Table 6 that out of 99 respondents working in state government, 81 (81.82 per cent) of them are OC, 12 (12.12 per cent) of them are BC/MBC and 6 (6.06 per cent) of them are SC/ST.

Out of 163 respondents working in public sector, 127 (77.91 per cent), 22 (13.50 per cent) and 14 (8.59 per cent) of them are OC, BC/BMBC and SC/ST respectively.

Table 6 also points out that out of 79 respondents working in private industrial sector, 61 (77.22 per cent) of them are OC, 13 (16.46 per cent) of them are BC/MBC and 5 (6.32 per cent) of them are SC/ST. Out of 58 respondents working in private service sector, 47 (81.03 per cent) of them are OC, 7 (12.07 per cent) of them are BC/MBC and 4 (6.90 per cent) of them are SC/ST.

Further, Table 7 also explains that out of 137 respondents working in the private sector, 108 (78.83 per cent), 20 (160 per cent) and 9 (6.57 per cent) of them are OC, BC/MBC and SC/ST respectively.

The distribution of women respondents according to their family size is given in Table 8.

Table 8
Family Size of The Sample Respondents

Family Size	*Public*			*Private*		
	Central	*State*	*Total*	*Industry*	*Service*	*Total*
Below 3	15 (23.44)	40 (40.40)	55 (33.74)	31 (39.24)	23 (39.66)	54 (39.42)
3-5	42 (65.63)	56 (56.57)	98 (60.12)	36 (45.57)	27 (46.55)	63 (45.98)
5 and above	7 (10.93)	3 (3.03)	10 (6.14)	12 (15.19)	8 (13.79)	20 (14.60)
Total	64 (100)	99 (100)	163 (100)	79 (100)	58 (100)	137 (100)

Source: Survey Data.
Figures in brackets denote percentages to total.

Table 8 clearly exhibits that, out of 64 respondents working in central government, 15 (23.44 per cent) of them have below 3 in the family, 42 (65.63 per cent) of hem have 3-5 and 7 (10.93 per cent) of them have 5 and above. Out of 99 respondents working in state government, 56 (56.57 per cent) of them have 3-5, 40 (40.40 per cent) of them have below 3 and 3 (3.03 per cent) of them have 5 and above family size. It also exhibits that out of 163 respondents, 98 (60.12 per cent), 55 (33.74 per cent) and 10 (6.14 per cent) of them have 3-5, below 3 and 5 and above respectively.

Further it is explicit that, out of 79 respondents working in private industry sector, 36 (45.47 per cent) of them have 3-5 family size, 31 (39.24 per cent) of them have below 3 and 12 (15.19 per cent) of them have 5 and above family size. Out of 58 sample respondents working in service sector, 27 (46.55) of them have 3-5, 23 (39.66 per cent) of them have below 3 and 8 (13.79 per cent) of them have 5 and above. It is also observed from the Table 7 that out of 137 respondents 63 (45.98 per cent), 54 (39.42 per cent) and 20 (14.60 per cent) of them have 3-5, below 3 and 5 and above respectively.

It is inferred from the Table 9 that out of 64 respondents working in central government, 43 (67.19 per cent) of them belong to joint family and 21 (32.81 per cent) of them belong to nuclear family. Out of 99 respondents working in state government, 83 (83.84 per cent) of them and 16 (16.16 per cent) of them belong to joint family and nuclear family respectively. It also exhibits that out 163 respondents working in public sector, 126 (77.30 per cent) of them and 37 (22.70 per cent) of them belong to joint family system and nuclear family respectively.

Table 9

Classification of The Respondents According to The Type of Family

Type of	*Public*			*Private*		
Family	*Central*	*State*	*Total*	*Industry*	*Service*	*Total*
Joint family	43 (67.19)	83 (83.84)	126 (77.10)	61 (77.22)	51 (87.93)	112 (81.75
Nuclear family	21 (32.81)	16 (16.16)	37 (22.70)	18 (22.78)	7 (12.07)	25 (18.25)
Total	64 (100)	99 (100)	163 (100)	79 (100)	58 (100)	137 (100)

Source: Survey Data.

Figures in brackets denote percentages to total.

The Table 9 also deduces that, out of 79 respondents working in industrial sector of private sector, 61 (77.22 per cent) of them belong to joint family and 18 (22.78 per cent) of them belong to nuclear family. Out of 58 respondents working in service sector, 51 (87.93 per cent) of them and 7 (12.07 per cent) of them belong to joint family and nuclear family respectively. It also explains that out of 137 respondents of private sector, 112 (81.75 per cent) of them and 25 (18.25 per cent) of them are belong to joint family and nuclear family respectively.

Table 10 deduced that out of 59 respondents working in public central government sector, 22 (37.29 per cent) of them come under the income category of below Rs.10,000 of their spouses, 21 (35.59

Table 10
Distribution of The Respondents According to their Spouses' Monthly Income

Income (Rs.)	*Public*			*Private*		
	Central	*State*	*Total*	*Industry*	*Service*	*Total*
Below 10000	22	35	57	36	23	59
	(37.29)	(39.77)	(38.78)	(50.00)	(42.59)	(46.83)
10000-15000	21	32	53	18	15	34
	(35.59)	(36.36)	(36.05)	(25.00)	(29.63)	(26.98)
15000 and	16	21	37	18	15	33
above	(27.12)	(23.87)	(25.17)	(25.00)	(27.78)	(26.19)
Total	59	88	147	72	54	126
	(100)	(100)	(100)	(100)	(100)	(100)

Note: Figures in brackets denote percentages to total.

per cent) of them are in the income group of Rs.10000-15000 and 16 (27.12 per cent) of them come under the group of income Rs.15,000 and above. Out of 88 respondents working in the state government, 35 (39.77 per cent) of them come under the income category of below Rs.10,000. 32 (36.36 per cent) of them and 21 (23.87 per cent) of them come under the income category of Rs.10000-15000 and 15000 and above respectively.

Further, it is also observed that out of 147 respondents of public sector, 57 (38.78 per cent) of them 58 (39.46 per cent) of them and 37 (25.17 per cent) of them one come under the income category of below 10,000, Rs.10,000-15,000 and Rs.15000 and above respectively.

In the case of private sector, out of 72 respondents, in industrial group, 36 (50 per cent) have spouses in Rs.10,000 per month category, 18 (25 per cent) each in income group of Rs.10000-15000 and Rs.15000 and above respectively. In service sector, out 54 respondents, majority of them (42.59 per cent) are under the category of below Rs.10,000, 16 (29.63 per cent) of them and 15 (27.7 per cent) of them belong to the income category of Rs.10000-15000 and Rs.15000 and above respectively.

In overall, out 126 respondents in private sector, 59 (46.83 per cent) of them have spouses who belong to the income group of below Rs.10000, 34 (26.98) of them come under the group of Rs.10000-15000 and remaining 33 (26.19) of them are in the income group of Rs.15000 and above.

Thus it is inferred from the analysis that 40-50 per cent of the respondents have spouses who belong to the category of income below Rs.10000 followed by the income category Rs.10000-15000.

Table 11 exhibits clearly the distribution of the respondents according to their family monthly income.

Table 11
Distribution of The Respondents by Their Family Monthly Income

Family	*Public*			*Private*		
Income (Rs.)	*Central*	*State*	*Total*	*Industry*	*Service*	*Total*
Below 15000	4	5	9	4	3	7
	(6.25)	(5.05)	(5.52)	(5.06)	(5.17)	(5.11)
15000-20000	23	36	59	21	20	41
	(35.94)	(36.37)	(36.20)	(26.58)	(34.48)	(29.93)
20000-25000	32	54	86	48	33	81
	(50.00)	(54.55)	(52.76)	(60.76)	(56.90)	(59.12)
25000 and	5	4	9	6	2	8
above	(50.00)	(4.04)	(5.52)	(7.59)	(3.45)	(5.84)
Total	64	99	163	79	58	137
	(100)	(100)	(100)	(100)	(100)	(100)

Source: Survey Data.
Figures in brackets denote percentages to total.

It is seen from Table 11 that out of 163 respondents working in public sector, a majority of the respondents (52.76 per cent) are having family income of Rs.20000-25000 per month. It is followed by the category Rs.15000-20000, 9 (5.52 per cent) of them each in group below Rs.15000 and Rs.20000 and above respectively.

Out of 64 respondents working in central government, 32 (50 per cent) of them are having the family income of Rs.20000-25000. It is followed by the income category Rs.15000-20000. In the case state government, out of 99 respondents, 54 (54.55 per cent) of them come under the category of Rs.20000-25000 of family income, 36 (36.37 per cent) of them are under the category of Rs.15000-20000 and 5 (5.05 per cent) of them and 4 (4.04 per cent) of them are having the family monthly income of below Rs.15000 and Rs.20000 and above respectively.

In the case of private sector, out of 137 respondents, 81 of them (59.12 per cent) are having the family monthly income of Rs.20000-25000, 41 (29.93 per cent) belong to Rs.15000-20000, 8 (5.84 per cent) of them only having Rs.25000 and above and remaining 7 (5.11 per cent) of them are having below Rs.15000.

Out 79 respondents in the industrial group under private sector, 48 of the (60.76 per cent) belong to the category of family income of Rs.2000-25000, 21 (26.58 per cent) of them are in the group of Rs.15000-20000, 6 (7.59 per cent) of them and 4 (5.06 per cent) of them belong to the family income category of below Rs.15000 and Rs.20000 and above respectively.

In the case of service group, out of 58 respondents, 33 (56.90 per cent) of them are under the family income category of Rs.20000-25000 followed by the category Rs.15000 and 20000 (34.48 per cent). Only 3 (5.17 per cent) and 2 (3.45 per cent) of them respectively belong to the category of below Rs.15000 and Rs.20000 and above.

Thus it is inferred from the analysis that majority of the respondents, 50 to 60 per cent, belong to the category of family monthly income of Rs.20000-25000.

RELATIONSHIP BETWEEN INCOME OF THE RESPONDENTS AND THEIR FAMILY CHARACTERISTICS

In this section, an attempt has been made to examine the relationship between the income of the respondents and their family characteristics namely family size, family income and spouses income.

In order to examine the relationship, chi-square test was used. It is calculated by adopting the following formula.

$$\text{Chi} - \text{Square} = \sum\frac{(O-E)^2}{E}$$

With (r-1) (e-1) degrees of freedom

Where

O – Observed frequency

E – Expected frequency

$$E = \frac{\text{Row total} \times \text{column total}}{\text{Grand Total}}$$

C = Number of column in a on ligancy fall

r = Number of rows contingency

Relationship between Family Size and Monthly Income

Women as daughters, wives, mothers and grandmothers have their own family responsibilities. If there are more number of members in the family, women take up an occupation either to enhance the family in one or to satisfy their own personal ambition. A two-way table is prepared to test the relationship between the income of the respondents and their family size. Table 12 exhibits the income of the respondents and their family size.

Table 12 shows that in the case of public sector out of 15 respondents whose monthly income is below Rs.5000, (6.67 per cent) of them fall under the family size below 3, 12 (80.0 per cent) of them fall between 3-5 and 2 (13.33 per cent) fall under the family size above 5. Out of 122 respondents where monthly income is between Rs.5000-Rs.10,000, 38 (31.15 per cent) of them come under family size below 3, 81 (66.39 per cent) of them have the family size between 3 to 5 and 3 (2.46 per cent) of then fall under the family size above 5. The respondents where monthly income is above Rs.10,000, out of 26, 16 (61.54 per cent) of them fall under family size below 3, 5 (19.23 per cent) of them have family size between 3 to 5 and 5 (19.23 per cent) of them fall under family size above 5.

In order to find out whether there is any correlation between the family size and income of respondents, chi-square test has been applied. The results of the Chi-square test are furnished below.

Calculated value of Chi-square	=	24.894
Table value at 5 per cent level	=	9.488
Degrees of freedom	=	4

As the calculated value of Chi-square is greater than the table value at 5 per cent level of significance, there is a relationship between income of the respondents and their family size in public sector.

In the case of private sector, out of 17 respondents where monthly income is below Rs.5000, 5 (29.42 per cent) of them have the family size below 3, 6 (35.29 per cent of them the family size between 3 to 5 and family size above 5. Out of 102 respondents where monthly income ranges between Rs.5000 – Rs.10,000, 43 (42.16 per cent) of them have the family size below 3, 50 (49.02 per cent) of them have family size between 3 to 5 and 9 (8.82 per cent) of them have family size above 5. Out of 18 respondents where monthly income is above

Table 12
Relationship Between Family Size and Monthly Income of The Respondents

Family	*Public*				*Private*			
Size	*Below Rs.5000*	*Rs.5000-10000*	*Rs.10000 and above*	*Total*	*Below Rs.5000*	*Rs.5000-10000*	*Rs.10000 and above*	*Total*
Below 3	1	38	16	55	5	43	6	54
	(6.67)	(31.15)	(61.54)	(33.74)	(29.42)	(42.16)	(33.33)	(39.42)
3-5	12	81	5	98	6	50	7	63
	(80.0)	(66.39)	(19.23)	(60.12)	(35.29)	(49.02)	(38.89)	(45.98)
5 and above	2	3	5	10	6	9	5	20
	(13.33)	(2.46)	(19.23)	(6.14)	(35.29)	(8.82)	(27.78)	(14.60)
Total	15	122	26	163	17	102	18	137
	(100)	(100)	(100)	(100)	(100)	(100)	(100)	(100)

Source: Survey Data.
Figures in brackets denote percentages to total.

Rs.10,000, 6 (33.33 per cent) have family size below 3, 7 (38.89 per cent) of them have family size between 3 to 5 and 5 (27.78 per cent) of them have family size above 5.

In order to know whether there is co-relation between the income of the respondents and their family size, Chi-square test was used. The results are given below.

Calculated value	=	13.4888
Table value at 5 per cent level	=	9.488
Degrees of freedom	=	4

Since the calculated value is greater than the table value of Chi-square at 5 per cent level, there exists a relationship between the income of the respondents and their family size in private sector.

Relationship between Monthly Income of the Respondents and Their Family Monthly Income

Table 13 presents the distribution of the respondents according to their monthly income and their family income.

Table 13 shows the relationship between family income and monthly income of the respondents. Out of 15 respondents where monthly income is below Rs.5000 in the case of public sector, 2 (13.33) have family income below Rs.15,000, 5(33.33 per cent) of them have family income between Rs.15000 – Rs.20,000. 6 (40.0 per cent) of them have family income between Rs.20,000 to Rs.25000 and 2 (13.33 per cent) of them have family income above Rs.25000. Out of 122 respondents where monthly income is between Rs.5000-Rs.10,000, 2 (6.56 per cent) of them have family income below Rs.15,000, 45 (36.88 per cent) of them have family income between Rs.15000-Rs.20,000, 70 (57.38 per cent) of them have family income between Rs.20,000 – Rs.25,000 and 5 (4.10 per cent) of them have family income above Rs.25,000. Out of 26 respondents where monthly income is above Rs.10,000. 5 (19.23 per cent) of them have family income below Rs.15000, 9 (34.62 per cent) of them have family income between Rs.15000-Rs.20,000, 10 (38.46 per cent) of them have family income between Rs.20000 – Rs. 25000 and 2 (7.69 per cent) of them family income above Rs.25000.

In order to find out whether there is any co-relation between the income of the respondents and their family income, Chi-square test was applied. The results are presented below:

Table 13

Relationship Between Monthly Income of The Respondents and Their Family Monthly Income

Family Income (in Rs.)	*Public*				*Private*			
	Below Rs.5000	*Rs.5000-10000*	*Rs.10000 and above*	*Total*	*Below Rs.5000*	*Rs.5000-10000*	*Rs.10000 and above*	*Total*
Below 15000	2 (13.33)	2 (6.56)	5 (19.23)	9 (5.52)	2 (11.76)	3 (2.94)	2 (11.11)	7 (5.11)
15000-20000	5 (33.33)	45 (36.88)	9 (34.62)	59 (36.20)	10 (58.82)	29 (28.43)	2 (11.11)	41 (29.93)
20000-25000	6 (40.0)	70 (57.38)	10 (38.46)	86 (52.76)	3 (17.65)	67 (65.69)	11 (61.11)	81 (59.12)
25000 and above	2 (13.33)	5 (4.10)	2 (7.69)	9 (5.52)	2 (11.76)	3 (2.94)	3 (6.67)	8 (5.84)
Total	15 (100)	122 (100)	26 (100)	163 (100)	17 (100)	102 (100)	18 (100)	137 (100)

Note: Figures in brackets denote percentages to total.

Calculated value	=	20.67
Table value at 5 per cent level	=	12.592
Degrees of freedom	=	6

As the calculated value is greater than the table value at 5 per cent level, there is a relationship between the income of the respondents and their family income.

In the case of private sector, out of 17 respondents where monthly income is below Rs.5000, 2 (11.76 per cent) of them have family income below Rs.15,0000, 10 (58.82 per cent) of them have family income between Rs.15000-Rs.20000, 3 (17.65 per cent) of them haven family income between Rs.20,000 – Rs.25000 and 2 (11.76 per cent) of them have family income above Rs. 25000. Out of 102 respondents where monthly income ranges between Rs.5000-Rs.10,000, 3 (2.94 per cent) of them have family income below Rs.15000, 29 (28.43 per cent) of them have family income between Rs.15000-Rs.20000, 67 (65.69 per cent) of them have family income between Rs.20000-Rs.25000 and 3 (2.94 per cent) of them have above Rs.25000. Out of 18 respondents where monthly income is above Rs.10,000, 2 (11.11 per cent) of them have family income below Rs.15000 and between Rs.15000-Rs.20000, 11 (61.11 per cent) of them have family income between Rs.20000-Rs.25000 and 3 (16.67 per cent) of them have family income above 25000.

To test the co-relation between the income of the respondents working in private sector and their family income, Chi-square test has been used. The computed results are given below.

Calculated value	=	12.950
Table value at 5 per cent level	=	12.592
Degrees of freedom	=	6

As the calculated Chi-square value is more than the table value at 5 per cent level of significance, there exists a relationship between the income of the respondents and their family income.

Relationship between Income of the Respondents and their Spouses Income

In order to test the relationship between the monthly income of the respondents and their spouse income, a two-way table is prepared and presented in Table 14.

Table 14

Comparison of Monthly Average Income between The Respondents and Their Spouse

Spouse's	*Public*				*Private*			
Income (in Rs.)	*Below Rs.5000*	*Rs.5000-10000*	*Rs.10000 and above*	*Total*	*Below Rs.5000*	*Rs.5000-10000*	*Rs.10000 and above*	*Total*
Below 10000	3 (20.0)	52 (46.85)	2 (9.52)	57 (38.78)	6 (37.5)	50 (52.63)	3 (20.0)	59 (46.83)
10000-15000	7 (46.67)	38 (34.23)	13 (61.90)	58 (39.46)	5 (31.25)	20 (21.05)	9 (60.0)	34 (26.98)
15000 and above	5 (33.33)	21 (18.92)	6 (28.57)	32 (21.77)	5 (31.25)	25 (26.32)	3 (20.0)	33 (26.19)
Total	15 (100)	111 (100)	21 (100)	147 (100)	16 (100)	95 (100)	15 (100)	126 (100)

Note: Figures in brackets denote percentages to total.

Table 14 shows the monthly average income between the respondents and spouse. In the case of public sector, out of 15 respondents where monthly income is below Rs.5000, 3 (20 per cent) of their spouses' income is below 10,000, 7 (46.67 per cent) of their spouses' income is between Rs.10000-Rs.15000 and 5 (33.33 per cent) of their spouses' income is above Rs.15000. Out of 111 respondents where monthly income is between Rs.5000-Rs.10,000, 52 (46.85 per cent) of their spouses' income is below Rs.10,000, 38 (34.23 per cent) is Rs.15000 and 21 (18.92 per cent) of their spouses' income in above Rs.15000. Out of 21 respondents whose monthly income is above Rs.10,000, 2 (9.52 per cent) of them have spouses' income below Rs.10,000, 13 (61.90 per cent) of them have spouses' income between Rs.10000-Rs.15000 and 6 (28.57 per cent) of them have spouses' income above Rs.15000.

In order to find out the relationship between the income of the respondents and their spouses' income, chi-square test was applied. The results are furnished below

Calculated value	=	15.14
Table value at 5 per cent level	=	9.488
Degrees of freedom	=	4

As the calculated value is greater them the table value at 5 per cent level, there exists a relationship between the income of the respondents and their spouses income.

In the case of private sector, out of 16 respondents whose monthly income is below Rs.5000, 6 (37.5 per cent) of them have spouses' income below Rs.10,000, 5 (31.25 per cent) of them have spouses' income between Rs.10000-Rs.15000 and above Rs.15000. Out of 95 respondents where monthly income is between Rs.5000 – Rs.10,000, 50 (52.63 per cent) of them have spouses' income below 10,000, 20 (21.05 per cent) of them spouses' income between 10,000-Rs.15000 and 25 (26.32 per cent) of them have spouses' income above Rs.15000. Out of 15 respondents where monthly income is above Rs.10,000, 3 (20.0 per cent) of them have their spouses income below Rs.10000 and above Rs.15000. Only 9 (60.0 per cent) of them have their spouses income between Rs.10000-Rs.15000.

To test whether there is any relationship between the income of the respondents and their spouses income, chi-square test has been applied. The results are given below:

Calculated value	=	5.9819
Table value at 5 per cent level	=	9.488
Degrees of freedom	=	4

As the calculated value is more than the table value at 5 per cent level of significance, there is a relation between the income of the respondents and their spouses income.

VARIATION IN MONTHLY INCOME BETWEEN DIFFERENT GROUPS OF WOMEN WORKERS

In this section, an attempt has been made to examine the variation in monthly income of women workers between public and private sector, central and state and industry and service groups. For this one way ANOVA was applied separately and the results are presented in Table 15, 16 and 17.

The results of Table 15 revealed that there was a significant variation in the monthly income of women workers between public and private sectors. Hence, it may be concluded that the monthly income varied significantly for sector among women workers.

Table 15
One-way Anova Test Results of Monthly Income among Women Workers in Public and Private Sector

Source of Variation	*Total Sum of Squares*	*Degrees of Freedom*	*Mean Sum of Squares*	*F- ratio*	*Table $F_{0.05}$*
Between groups	489720	1	489720	6.86*	3.84
Within group	21271240	298	71380		
Total	21760960	299			

* Significant at 5 per cent level.

Table 16
One-way Anova Test Results of Monthly Income among Women Workers in Central and State Under Public Sector

Source of Variation	*Total Sum of Squares*	*Degrees of Freedom*	*Mean Sum of Squares*	*F- ratio*	*Table $F_{0.05}$*
Between groups	394860	7	394860	6.20*	3.84
Within group	10257310	161	63710		
Total	10652170	162			

* Significant at 5 per cent level.

Table 17
One-way Anova Test Results of Monthly Income among Women Workers in Industry and Service Group under Private Sector

Source of Variation	*Total Sum of Squares*	*Degrees of Freedom*	*Mean Sum of Squares*	*F- ratio*	*Table $F_{0.05}$*
Between groups	347320	1	347320	5.95*	3.84
Within group	7878600	135	58360		
Total	8225920	136			

* Significant at 5 pent level.

The results of one-way ANOVA test for women workers in central and state government are presented in Table 16.

It is revealed from Table 16 that there was a significant variation in the monthly income between central and state women employees working in public sector. Hence, in may be concluded that the monthly income varied significantly between Central and State.

Table 17 exhibits the results of one-way ANOVA test for women working in private sector.

It is inferred from the results of Table 17 that the difference in the monthly income between industrial and service group was statistically significant at 5 per cent level. Thus it may be concluded that the monthly income varied significantly for different groups among women in private sector.

ANALYSIS OF WOMEN WORKER CONTRIBUTION TOWARDS FAMILY INCOME

In order to assess the contribution of women workers to family income, the following mathematical formulations were used for multiple regression analysis,

$$\text{Log } Y = \beta_0 + \beta_1 \log X_1 + \beta_2 \log X_2 + u$$

Where,

Y = Total family income in (rupees)
X_1 = Earnings of women workers (in rupees)
X_2 = Earning of their spouses (in rupees)
U = Error term or unexplained variation of total family income associated with the left out variables.

β_0, β_1 and β_2 are the parameters to be estimated.

The above model was estimated separately for women work participants of the public and private sectors by the method of least squares. The estimated results are presented in Table 18 and 19.

Table 18
Estimated Regression Results for Women Workers in Public Sector

Variable	*Centre*	*State*	*Overall*
Intercept	1.3212	1.7516	1.4816
X_1	0.0917*	0.0812*	0.0866*
	(3.0142)	(2.9271)	(3.6972)
X_2	0.0938*	0.0799*	0.0851*
	(3.6972)	(4.0171)	(3.1471)
R^2	0.8016	0.7763	0.7912
F – value	132.74	96.72	118.71
No. of observations	59	88	147

Figures in brackets represent t-values
* Indicates that the coefficients are statistically significant at 5 per cent level.

Table 19
Estimated Regression Results for Women Workers in Private Sector

Variable	*Centre*	*State*	*Overall*
Intercept	1.0716	1.3247	1.1873
X_1	0.0654*	0.0597*	0.0617*
	(4.6231)	(3.7962)	(4.1234)
X_2	0.0723*	0.0687*	0.0698*
	(5.6761)	(4.9214)	(5.1061)
R^2	0.7569	0.7149	0.7371
F – value	138.16	108.74	121.36
No. of observations	72	54	126

Figures in brackets represent t- values
* Indicates that the co-efficents are statistically significant at 5 per cent level.

It could be observed from Table 18 that the independent variables included in the model for centre, state and overall public sector have indicated 77 to 80 per cent variations in total family income. In the case of centre, the co-efficient of multiple determination (R^2) was 0.8016 indicating 80.16 per cent variation in total income. The regression co-efficients of variables namely earnings of women workers and their spouses' earnings were statistically significant at 5 per cent level. One unit increase in these variables could increase the total family income by 0.0917 per cent and 0.0938 per cent respectively.

In the case of state women workers, two independent variables are jointly responsible for 77.63 per cent of total family income. The co-efficients of earnings of women workers and their spouses were statistically significant at 5 per cent level. It implies that one unit increase in these variables may lead to 0.0812 per cent and 0.0799 per cent increase in total family income.

In overall public sector, R^2 indicates that 79.12 per cent variations are explained by the two independent variables included in the model. Both the variables were statistically significant at 5 per cent level. It means that an additional unit of these variables could increase total family income by 0.0866 per cent and 0.0851 per cent respectively. The F value indicates that estimated regression model is statistically significant at one per cent in three cases.

Table 19 shows the estimated values of regression equations for industry, service and overall category of private sector.

Table 19 reveals that in the case of industry under private sectors, all the variables included in the regression model jointly explain about 75.69 per cent variations in total family income. The regression co-efficients of variables namely earnings of women workers and earnings of their spouses were statistically significant at 5 per cent level. It indicates that an addition unit in these variables could increase total family income by 0.0654 per cent and 0.0723 per cent respectively.

In the case of service, R_2 value was 0.7149 indicating 71.49 per cent variation in total family income. The co-efficient of earnings of women workers and earnings of their spouses were statistically significant at 5 per cent level. It means that one unit increase in these variables may effect 0.0597 per cent and 0.0687 per cent increase in total family income.

In overall private sector, R^2 indicates that 73.71 per cent variations in the dependent variable are explained by all the explanatory variables. The variables namely earnings of women workers and earnings of their spouses were statistically significant at 5 per cent level. It implies that for one unit increase in these variables, total family income could be increased by 0.0617 per cent and 0.0698 per cent respectively. As per F value given in Tables 2, the regression model fitted is found to be significant at one percent level in three cases.

Thus it may be concluded from the analysis that the contribution of women workers towards family income is more than the earnings of their spouses. Therefore, the earnings of women workers contribute significantly towards family income.

The findings of the chapter may be summarised as follows:

It has been found that more than 45 per cent of the respondents belong to the age group of 30-40 years in both public as well as in private sectors. Majority of respondents (45 per cent) have accomplished S.S.L.C./PUC and 35 per cent are graduates. Majority of 91.97 per cent of the respondents are married. Majority of the women respondents' monthly income has been in the range of Rs.5,000 to Rs.10,000 in the study area.

The family size, family income and spouses' income have influenced the income of the respondent both in public and private sector. The result of ANOVA test revealed that the monthly income of the respondents varied significantly among sectors, Central and State Government under public sector and industry and services group under private sector.

The regression analysis revealed that the contribution of women workers towards family income is more than the earnings of their spouses.

5

WORK–FAMILY CONFLICT, QUALITY OF WORK LIFE AND JOB SATISFACTION

The concept of quality of working life (QWL) which refers to a relationship between the worker and work environment, gained importance, since an effort has been taken to improve QWL of women work participation in both public and private sectors. Job satisfaction is believed to be one important aspect of QWL and to study QWL should also have a consideration for job satisfaction and work-family conflict. Hence, the present study attempts to achieve the following objectives:

1. Analysing and comparing the work-family conflict of women employees in public and private sector.
2. Assessing the contribution of independent variables to quality of work life of women employees.

MEASUREMENT OF WORK-FAMILY CONFLICT VARIABLES

The work-family conflict variables have been identified in order to study the relationship between levels of job satisfaction and work-family conflict of women employees working in public and private sectors. Each of the ten variables is measured with the help of responses to relevant questions in respect to each construct by using a four point scaling technique. (Vide Appendix).

Each statement/question incorporated in the interview schedule under work-family conflict had four alternative responses namely 'Always', "Usually', 'Sometimes' and 'ever', To attain the score, o was given to 'Always' 1 to 'Usually', 2 to 'Sometimes' and 3 to 'Never' for the constructs namely work involvement, family involvement, work expectations, family expectations, quality of work life, quality of family life and life satisfaction. A score of 3 was given to 'Always', 2 to 'Usually', 1 to 'Sometimes' and 0 to 'Never' for the constructs, work conflict, family conflict and work-family conflict.

There were about thirty-two statements under the work-family conflict construct. Work involvement, work expectations, family involvement, family expectations, work conflict and family conflict are assessed with two statements each and the score values range from 0 to 6. Work-family conflict is assessed by eight statements and the score values range from 0 to 24. Quality of work life, quality of family life and life satisfaction are assessed separately with four statements and the score values range from 0 to 12.

With the score values of each variable of work-family conflict, an attempt has been made to compare each variable with different sectors. For this purpose, mean score of each variable has been used and the difference in mean score values between sectors were examined by using t-test.

With a view to examine the internal consistency of ten variables of work-family conflict, standard deviation technique has been used. Internal consistency means stability of various variables within the group. The values of standard deviations of each variable have been calculated and compared with different sectors.

Further, correlation co-efficient technique has been used to analyse the relationship among the variables, which is compared with different levels of job satisfaction.

Two way ANOVA was carried out to examine the significant variation in quality of work life and job satisfaction of the women employees working in different type of organizations and income.

In order to assess the contribution of independent variables to quality of work life, step wise regression analysis was applied.

Likert scaling technique was used for measuring overall job satisfaction. The scale had 14 items and each item was presented n five point scale.

Analysis of Work-family Conflict

In order to examine the differences in mean score values of each variable of work-family conflict, the computed mean score values and t-values are presented in Table 1.

Table 1
Mean Score Value of Work-family Conflict Variables According to Sector Wise

SL. No.	*Variables*	*Public*	*Private*	*t-value*
1.	Work involvement	5.76	5.99	4.71*
2.	Work expectation	5.70	5.93	5.01*
3.	Work conflict	5.13	5.14	1.06
4.	Family involvement	5.55	4.69	3.92*
5.	Family expectation	5.49	5.06	2.96*
6.	Family conflict	5.05	5.0	1.16
7.	Work-family conflict	21.11	20.66	4.18*
8.	Quality of work life	12.64	11.90	4.68*
9.	Quality of family life	11.02	10.84	1.26
10.	Life satisfaction	10.90	11.26	1.26

It is revealed from Table 1 that out of ten variables, work involvement and work expectation have received higher mean score value from the private sector women employees. Family involvement, family expectation, work-family conflict, quality of working life and quality of family life have been given greater importance by the women working in public sector. The differences in mean values of work involvement, work expectation, family involvement, family expectation, work-family conflict and quality of working life between public and private sector women employees were statistically significant at 5 per cent level. It is inferred that the public sector women employees are highly associated with family involvement, family expectations, work family conflict and quality of working life whereas in the case of private sector employees, they are highly associated with work involvement and work expectation.

Table 2 shows the mean score values of work-family conflict variables of women employees working in different type of organizations in public and private sectors.

It is inferred from Table 2 that all the ten variables of work-family conflict have received higher mean values from the central government women employees compared to state government

Table 2
Mean Score Value of Work-family Conflict Variables According to Group Wise Public and Private Sector

SL. No.	*Variables*	*Public*			*Private*		
		Central	*State*	*t-value*	*Industry*	*Service*	*t-value*
1.	Work involvement	5.88	5.69	3.16*	6.00	5.98	5.12*
2.	Work expectation	5.73	5.69	1.06	5.96	5.88	1.26
3.	Work conflict	5.17	5.10	1.27	5.16	5.12	1.11
4.	Family involvement	5.66	5.48	1.04	5.07	4.18	3.96*
5.	Family expectation	5.59	5.42	3.16*	5.12	4.98	1.31
6.	Family conflict	5.11	5.01	1.32	5.01	4.99	1.01
7.	Work-family conflict	22.63	20.12	3.72*	21.31	19.78	3.16*
8.	Quality of work life	14.63	11.36	5.16*	12.47	11.12	3.98*
9.	Quality of family life	11.66	10.61	3.16*	11.36	10.12	1.08
10.	Life satisfaction	11.48	10.52	0.98	11.74	10.61	1.02

employees in public sector. The differences in mean values of the variables namely work involvement, family expectations, quality of work life and quality of family life between central and state government women employees were statistically significant. It indicates that central government employees are highly associated with family involvement, family expectations, quality of work life and quality of family life than the state government employees.

In the case of private sector, the mean values of all the ten variables of work-family conflict were found to be higher for industry compared to service in private sector. The significant differences in the mean values were found in work involvement, family involvement, work family conflict, and quality of work life. It means that women in industry are found to be associated more with work involvement, family involvement, work-family conflict and quality of work life than women in service category.

In order to examine the internal consistency of the variables, the calculating values of standard deviation are given in Table 3.

It is inferred from Table 3 that the value of standard deviation was found less in quality of work life, work conflict, work involvement work expectation and family involvement. These variables have shown higher level internal consistency among women employees working

Table 3
Internal Consistency of Work-family Conflict Variables with Sector Wise

SL. No.	*Variables*	*Public*			*Private*		
		Central	*State*	*Overall*	*Industry*	*Service*	*Overall*
1.	Work involvement	1.81	2.31	1.11	2.13	3.12	2.55
2.	Work expectation	2.32	3.14	1.62	4.28	3.92	4.13
3.	Work conflict	1.43	5.12	6.01	2.16	1.98	2.08
4.	Family involvement	2.94	3.12	4.05	3.12	2.96	3.05
5.	Family expectation	6.17	2.42	3.89	2.16	3.11	2.56
6.	Family conflict	5.82	4.92	7.27	4.12	3.16	3.71
7.	Work-family conflict	7.41	10.16	9.08	5.12	4.94	5.04
8.	Quality of work life	1.13	3.16	1.36	6.27	5.62	5.99
9.	Quality of family life	4.12	5.72	5.09	7.18	6.74	6.99
10.	Life satisfaction	5.62	6.12	5.92	3.62	3.12	3.41

S.D. – Standard Deviation.

in central government. In the case of state government then variables namely, work involvement and family expectation have a higher level of consistency than other variables among the women employees. In overall, pubic sector, a higher internal consistency is exhibited by the variables work involvement, quality of work life and work expectation. Thus it is inferred from the analysis that work involvement, work expectation and quality of work life have shown a higher level of consistency among women employees in public sector.

In the case of private sector, work involvement, work conflict and family expectation have shown a higher level of internal consistency among women employees in industry. Among women employees in service, a higher internal consistency is exhibited by the variables work conflict and family involvement. In overall of private sector, consistency among women employees was found in the variables work conflict, work involvement and family expectations. Thus it is inferred from the analysis that work involvement and work conflict have shown higher level internal consistency.

The calculated values of correlation co-efficient among the work-family conflict variables of women employees in central government are given in Table 4.

It is seen from Table 4 that there was a positive correlation among the variables namely work involvement, work expectations, family involvement, family expectations, work conflict, family conflict, and

Table 4
Correlations of Work-family Conflict Variables of Women Employees – Central

SL. No.	*Constructs*	*1*	*2*	*3*	*4*	*5*	*6*	*7*	*8*	*9*	*10*
1.	Work involvement	–									
2.	Work expectation	0.431	–								
3.	Work conflict	0.579	0.541*	–							
4.	Family involvement	0.323	0.409	0.451	–						
5.	Family expectation	0.309	0.673*	0.721*	0.618*	–					
6.	Family conflict	0.417	0.502	0.637*	0.513	0.431	–				
7.	Work-family conflict	0.619*	0.639	0.412	0.439	0.578*	0.609	–			
8.	Quality of work life	-0.721*	-0.398	-0.359	-0.342	-0.430	-0.329	-0.483*	–		
9.	Quality of family life	-0.531*	-0.419	-0.521	-0.547*	-0.518	-0.569	-0.511	0.673*	–	
10.	Life satisfaction	-0.316	-0.333	-0.418	0.703*	-0.612	-0.719	-0.461	-0.568	-0.421	–

* Indicates the Co-efficent is statistically significant at 5 per cent level.

work family conflict. It means that any change in these variables would cause changes in other variables in the same direction.

There was a negative correlation between the variables work involvement and quality of work life and quality of family life. It indicates that any change in these variables may bring in negative involvement in work. High correlation (more than 0.5) was found in many cases.

Computed results of correlation co-efficient of work-family conflict variables of women employees in state government are presented in Table 5.

It could be inferred from the results of Table 5 that correlations of the constructs of work family conflict of state employees are similar to those of employees with central government.

Thus, it is concluded from the analysis that as far as women employees in public sectors are concerned, the correlations among the variables of work-family conflict are the same.

The calculated values of correlation co-efficient in respect of work family conflict variables of women employees working in public sectors are presented in Table 6.

Table 6 shows that the correlation of work involvement with work conflict, and work-family conflict is high. Similarly the relationship of family involvement with work expectations, family expectations, work conflict, and family conflict is high (more than 0.5). The correlation between family expectations and family involvement, family expectation, and work family conflict is more than 0.5. Further the Table 6 shows that the relationship of quality of work life and work conflict and family conflict is negative. It implies that, any change in work conflict and family conflict would cause changes in quality of work life in the opposite direction.

The computed correlation co-efficients among the variables of work family conflict of women working in industry in private sector are presented in Table 7.

It is inferred from Table 7 that there is a positive correlation among the variables, namely work involvement, work expectations, family involvement, family expectations, work conflict, family conflict, work-family conflict and quality of family life. It shows that any change in these variables effects change in other variables in the same direction in the case of women employees working in industry.

Table 5
Correlations of Work-family Conflict Variables of Women Employees - State

SL. No.	*Constructs*	*1*	*2*	*3*	*4*	*5*	*6*	*7*	*8*	*9*	*10*
1.	Work involvement	–									
2.	Work expectation	0.213	–								
3.	Work conflict	0.359	0.421*	–							
4.	Family involvement	0.238	0.341	0.388	–						
5.	Family expectation	0.306	0.578*	0.599*	0.547*	–					
6.	Family conflict	0.413	0.428	0.563*	0.417	0.313	–				
7.	Work-family conflict	0.469*	0.513	0.318	0.354	0.462*	0.486	–			
8.	Quality of work life	-0.521*	-0.269	-0.263	-0.253	-0.333	-0.288	-0.698*	–		
9.	Quality of family life	-0.398*	-0.374	-0.429	-0.463*	-0.464	-0.449*	-0.461	0.618*	–	
10.	Life satisfaction .	-0.219	-0.282	-0.318	-0.599*	-0.578	-0.585	-0.386	-0.453	-0.328	–

* Indicates the Co-efficent is statistically significant at 5 per cent level.

Table 6
Correlations of Work-family Conflict Variables of Women Employees - Public Sector

SL. No.	*Constructs*	*1*	*2*	*3*	*4*	*5*	*6*	*7*	*8*	*9*	*10*
1.	Work involvement	–									
2.	Work expectation	0.429	–								
3.	Work conflict	0.488	0.632	–							
4.	Family involvement	0.526*	0.548	0.732*	–						
5.	Family expectation	0.348	0.563	0.638	0.568	–					
6.	Family conflict	0.518	0.392	0.467	0.643*	0.439	–				
7.	Work-family conflict	0.699*	0.332	0.461	0.505	0.646*	0.573	–			
8.	Quality of work life	-0.482	-0.503	-0.474	-0.501	-0.619*	-0.712*	-0.497*	–		
9.	Quality of family life	0.666	0.709*	0.459	0.732*	0.473	0.399	0.468	0.618*	–	
10.	Life satisfaction	-0.617	-0.729*	-0.549	-0.689*	-0.618*	-0.461	-0.321	-0.673*	-0.518*	–

* Indicates the Co-efficent is statistically significant at 5 per cent level.

Table 7
Correlations of Work-family Conflict Variables of Women Employees – Industry

SL. No.	Constructs	1	2	3	4	5	6	7	8	9	10
1.	Work involvement	–									
2.	Work expectation	0.561	–								
3.	Work conflict	0.312	0.569*	–							
4.	Family involvement	0.502	0.482	0.631*	–						
5.	Family expectation	0.593*	0.469	0.532	0.665*	–					
6.	Family conflict	0.421	0.471	0.641	0.379	0.315	–				
7.	Work-family conflict	0.637*	0.427	0.388	0.613*	0.401	0.521	–			
8.	Quality of work life	-0.293	-0.341	-0.389	-0.381	-0.461	-0.503	-0.561*	–		
9.	Quality of family life	0.587*	0.609	0.498	0.376	0.401	0.299	0.588	0.457	–	
10.	Life satisfaction	-0.463	-0.256	-0.470	-0.263	-0.561*	-0.559*	-0.481	-0.698*	-0.312	–

* Indicates the Co-efficent is statistically significant at 5 per cent level.

It is inferred from Table 7 that there is a negative correlation between quality of work life and other variables except quality of family life. The relationship between life satisfaction and other variables bears negative correlation. It indicates that all the variables, which influence work-family conflict, are inversely related to life satisfaction of women employees working in industries.

Computed results of correlation co-efficient of work-family conflict variables of women employees working in service sectors are presented in Table 8.

It is clear from Table 8 that the correlation co-efficient in respect of work family conflict constructs of women employees of service sector is similar to those of employees working in industry.

The results of correlation co-efficient of work family conflict variables of women employees of private sector of job satisfaction are presented in Table 9.

It is observed from Table 9 that there is a high positive correlation between work involvement and other constructs namely work expectations, family involvement, family expectations, work conflict, family conflict and work, family conflict. The same trend is found in the case of work expectations with other constructs except quality of family life and life satisfaction. The variables quality of work life, and life satisfaction correlate negatively with other work, family variables of women employees in private sector. It indicates that any changes in these variables effect opposite changes in other variables.

Thus it may be concluded from the analysis that the relationship among the variables of work-family conflict of women employees working in private sector is the same.

Analysis of Perceptions of Quality of Work Life (QWL) and Job Satisfaction

This section attempts to examine the significance in variations of quality of work life (QWL) of women employees according to organization and income. For this, a two-way ANOVA test was carried out and results are given for public sector and private sector in Tables 10 and 11.

Table 8

Correlations of Work-family Conflict Constructs of Women Employees – Service

SL. No.	Constructs	1	2	3	4	5	6	7	8	9	10
1.	Work involvement	–									
2.	Work expectation	0.612*	–								
3.	Work conflict	0.471	0.556*	–							
4.	Family involvement	0.421	0.592*	0.528	–						
5.	Family expectation	0.512*	0.436	0.371	0.460	–					
6.	Family conflict	0.319	0.527	0.416	0.352	0.586*	–				
7.	Work-family conflict	0.251	0.461*	0.349	0.374	0.321	0.429	–			
8.	Quality of work life	-0.409	-0.329	-0.330	-0.381	-0.491	-0.491	-0.601*	–		
9.	Quality of family life	-0.658*	-0.589*	-0.673*	-0.526*	-0.694*	-0.652*	-0.576*	0.698*	–	
10.	Life satisfaction	-0.303	-0.371	-0.567*	-0.552*	-0.421	-0.507	-0.389	-0.470	-0.270	–

* Indicates the Co-efficent is statistically significant at 5 per cent level.

Table 9

Correlations of Work-family Conflict Variables of Women Employees – Industry

SL. No.	*Constructs*	*1*	*2*	*3*	*4*	*5*	*6*	*7*	*8*	*9*	*10*
1.	Work involvement	–									
2.	Work expectation	0.630*	–								
3.	Work conflict	0.572*	0.551*	–							
4.	Family involvement	0.643*	0.597*	0.483	–						
5.	Family expectation	0.627*	0.674*	0.634*	0.397	–					
6.	Family conflict	0.598*	0.615*	0.676*	0.312	0.515	–				
7.	Work-family conflict	0.521*	0.619*	0.428	0.571*	0.653*	0.498*	–			
8.	Quality of work life	-0.490*	-0.438	-0.525*	-0.596*	-0.428	-0.317	-0.491*	–		
9.	Quality of family life	0.317	-0.364	-0.427	-0.472	-0.500	-0.628*	-0.430	0.671*	–	
10.	Life satisfaction	-0.373	-0.354	-0.671*	-0.637	-0.271	-0.518*	-0.687*	-0.318	-0.401	–

* Indicates the Co-efficent is statistically significant at 5 per cent level.

Table 10
Two-way Anova for Quality of Work Life According to Organisations (Central and State) and Income of The Respondents Working in Public Sector

Source of Variation	*Sum of Square*	*Degrees of Freedom*	*Mean Square*	*F-Value*	*Table $F_{0.05}$*
Main Effects					
Income	4828.16	1	4828.16	42.26*	3.84
Organizations	3421.82	2	1710.91	14.98*	3.00
Two way interactions	378.36	3	126.12	1.10	2.60
Residual or error	17821.72	156	114.24		
Total	26450.06	162			

* Significant at 5 per cent level.

Table 11
Two-way Anova for Quality of Work Life according to Organisations (Industry and Service) and Income of The Respondents Working in Private Sector

Source of Variation	*Total Sum of Square*	*Degrees of Freedom*	*Mean Sum of Square*	*F-Value*	*Table $F_{0.05}$*
Main Effects					
Income	4622.31	1	4622.31	36.57*	3.84
Organizations	3374.36	2	1687.18	13.35*	3.00
Two way interactions	366.71	3	122.24	0.97	2.60
Residual or error	16432.63	130	126.40		
Total	24796.01	136			

* Significant at 5 per cent level.

It is observed from Table 10 that though the two-way interaction was not significant, both the main effects, income and sectors were statistically significant at 5 per cent level. It indicates the respondents' perception of QWL differ according to income and sector. Perception of quality of working life scores of the women workers in public sector was significantly higher than that of the women workers in private sector (Vide Table 1). Quality of work life was significantly higher among the women of having central government income than the women of having state government income.

It is inferred from Table 11 that both the main effect, that is, income and organizations were statistically significant at 5 per cent level. The significant results suggest that the perception of QWL differ according to the type of organization and income. The perception of QWL score was found high in industry than in service sector. The perception was also different among the women having income from industry and service sector. But there was no joint effect (income and organizations) on quality of working life.

Table 12 and 13 exhibit the results of ANOVA test for examining the perceptions of job satisfaction according to organizations and income in public and private sectors respectively.

It is observed from Table 12 that there was no joint effect (income and organizations) on job satisfaction but the women workers differed according to income and type of organizations. The perception of

Table 12
Two-way Anova for Job Satisfaction according to Organisations (Central and State) and Income of The Respondents Working in Public Sector

Source of Variation	*Sum of Square*	*Degrees of Freedom*	*Mean Sum of Square*	*F-Value*	*Table $F_{0.05}$*
Main Effects					
Income	1322.16	1	1322.16	64.09*	3.84
Organizations	948.13	2	474.07	22.98*	3.00
Two way interactions	131.33	3	433.78	2.12	2.60
Residual or error	3218.61	156	20.63		
Total	5620.23	162			

* Significant at 5 per cent level.

Table 13
Two-way Anova for Job Satisfaction According to Organisations (Industry and Service) and Income of The Respondents Working in Private Sector

Source of Variation	*Total Sum of Square*	*Degrees of Freedom*	*Mean Sum of Square*	*F-Value*	*Table $F_{0.05}$*
Main Effects					
Income	1072.31	1	1072.31	44.04*	3.84
Sectors	841.71	2	420.86	17.28*	3.00
Two way interactions	162.36	3	54.12	2.22	2.60
Residual or error	3165.93	130	24.35		
Total	5242.31	136			

* Significant at 5 per cent level.

job satisfaction was significantly higher among the women working in central government job than the women of state government. Further job satisfaction was significantly higher for women of central government than the women in state government.

It is observed from Table 13 that the two way interaction was not significant indicating there was no joint effect on job satisfaction. The main effects (i.e the income and type of organizations) were significant. It means that the perception of job satisfaction differs according to the type of organization and income of different sectors.

Step Wise Regression Analysis

In order to assess the contribution of independent variables to quality of work life, step-wise regression analysis was carried out. In the regression model, three variables were introduced and the order of inclusion was as follows. Job satisfaction, quality of family life and monthly income. The computed results of step wise multiple regression are presented in Table 14.

Table 14
Step Wise Multiple Regression Dependent Variable Quality of Work Life (QWL)

Variables	*Multiple R*	R^2	*F*	*P*	*Beta*
Job satisfaction	0.9651	0.94	362.17	0.001	0.96
Quality of family life	0.9712	0.95	267.32	0.001	0.33
Income	0.9792	0.97	312.36	0.001	0.07

It is revealed from Table 14 that three of the variables were entered into the equation and the order of inclusion was as follows: Job satisfaction, quality of family life and income. As each of the additionals was entered, the multiple R and R^2 increased. This indicates that job satisfaction quality of family life and income were the best set of predictors of quality of work life having a combined contribution of about 97 per cent. Allowing one of the independent variables to operate, while controlling the other variables in equation, revealed that it was job satisfaction which had the highest contribution to quality of work followed by quality of family life and income respectively.

The findings of the chapter may be summarized as follows.

Women employees working in public sector have higher family involvement and family expectation whereas women working in private sector have higher work involvement and work expectation. The work-family conflict and quality of work life were found higher in the case of public sector than in private sector women employees.

In public sector, central government employees have higher work involvement, family expectation, work-family conflict, quality of work life and quality of family life than state government employees. In the case of private sector, employees in industry have higher work involvement, family involvement, work-family conflict and quality of work life, than women employees in service category.

The higher level of internal consistency among women employees was found in variables, work involvement and quality of work life, in the case of public sector; whereas, in the case of private sector, work conflict and work involvement have higher internal consistency.

Correlations among the variables of work-family conflict showed that work involvement and work conflict were found to have a positive relationship with work-family conflict in the case of public sector women employees. Quality of work life is negatively related with work-family conflict of the women employees working in central, state and overall.

In the case of industry, positive relationship was found between work-family conflict and other variable namely family expectation. Work-family conflict correlated positively with work expectation in the case of service category. In overall, private sector, a positive correlation was found between work-family conflict and the variables namely work involvement, work expectation, family expectation, work conflict and family conflict quality of work was inversely related with work-family conflict of women employees working in industry, service and overall.

Two-way Anova results revealed that both public and private sector women employees differ significantly in the perception of quality of work life according to their income and types of organizations. They also differ in the perception of job satisfaction according to their income and organizations.

Step wise multiple regression results revealed that the job satisfaction had a greater contribution to quality of work life.

6

WOMEN WORK PARTICIPATION AND EMPOWERMENT THROUGH DECISION MAKING

Different individuals have used different methodologies of empowerment. Radhakrishna Rao (2001) suggested a triangular model of empowerment. Mayoux (1998) objected to the conventional methodology of empowerment and suggested a framework for analyzing women's empowerment. These studies indicate that empowerment encompasses a wide variety of factors–economic, political and social. The present study makes an attempt to analyse the following objectives:

1. Analysing the extent to which women work participation empower them through decision-making.
2. Examining the factors which influence the empowerment of working women in public and private sector.

Economic empowerment of women is mainly based on their participation in decision making process with regard to raising and distribution of income, investments and expenditure at all levels. The entire efforts of empowering women are to help them to exercise their rights in decision making at all levels and in every sphere, both within and outside the households as equal partners in the society. Efforts are on to enhance the capacity of women to earn and ensure that they get access to and control/ownership of all family/community assets.

THE ANALYTICAL FRAME WORK

The empowerment of women in the present study has been measured in terms of their decision making capacity which has been classified on the basis of self, myself more than husband/family member. Both equal, husband/family member more than myself and husband/family member. These five aspects are applicable for seven variables which are identified for measuring the decision making power of women. The identified variables are (i) preparation of the family budget (ii) education of children (iii) health and medicine (iv) leisure activities (v) purchase of home appliances (vi) giving away gifts to others and vii) personal needs. The responses have been obtained from the sample women work participants in five aspects for each variable. The responses observed for each variable have been scored. To secure the total empowerment score of a woman work participant, five points are given for "self", 4 points for "myself more than husband/family/member", three points are given for "both equal", two points for husband/family member more than myself and one point for 'husband/family member" responses. Thus the total empowerment score of a respondent is obtained by adding up the scores of all 7 variables.

One way ANOVA was carried out to examine whether women working in different sectors have caused significant variation in empowerment.

The level of empowerment has been classified into three categories namely low level, medium level and high level for analytical purposes. While the score values $\geq \overline{X} + SD$ and the score values $\leq \overline{X} - SD$ have been classified as high level empowerment and low level empowerment respectively, the score values between $\overline{X} + SD$ and $\overline{X} - SD$ have been classified as medium level empowerment, $\overline{X}$ and SD are the arithmetic mean and standard deviation calculated from the score values.

In order to examine the relationship between the level of empowerment and socio economic factors, the chi-square test has been employed. It is calculated by adopting the following formula (Kothari, 1978).

$$\text{Chi-square} = \Sigma \frac{(O-E)^2}{E}$$

With $(r\text{-}1)$ $(c\text{-}1)$ degrees of freedom.

Where,

O = Observed frequency

E = Expected frequency

$$E = \frac{\text{Row Total} \times \text{Column Total}}{\text{Grand Total}}$$

C = number of rows in a contingency table

R = number of columns in a contingency table

In order to assess the contribution of independent variables to women empowerment, step wise multiple regression analysis was carried out.

ANALYSIS OF EMPOWERMENT THROUGH DECISION MAKING

This section attempts to analyse the decision making power enjoyed by women work participants on the variables namely (i) preparation of the family budget (ii) education of children (iii) purchase of property (iv) purchase of furniture (v) purchase of home appliances (vi) giving away gifts to others and (vii) personal needs.

Family Budgeting

Family budgeting here refers to the various items to be purchased, duty and the amount of money to been spent on each item, variation in the terms of consumption and the like. The decision making of women work participants on preparation of the family budget is presented in Table 1.

It is inferred from Table 1 that nearly 50 per cent of the women working in public sector and 32.85 per cent in private sector take independent decisions relating to the family budget. Independent decision making was found less in private sector when compared to public sector. Joint discussions were taken by 40.49 per cent of families in the case of public sector while their percentage was 54.02 per cent in private sector. Husband or family member alone taking decision was 9.82 per cent in public sector and 13.14 per cent in private sector. Thus, it is inferred from the total some that majority of working women could take decisions independently relating to family budget.

Table 1
Decision Making on Preparation of The Family Budget

Sl.No.	*Final Decision Taken*	*Public*		*Private*	
		Number of Respondents	*Total Score*	*Number of Respondents*	*Total Score*
1.	Self	81 (49.69)	405	45 (32.85)	225
2.	Myself more than husband /family member	26 (15.95)	104	13 (9.49)	52
3.	Both equal	22 (13.50)	66	38 (27.74)	114
4.	Husband / family member more than myself	18 (11.04)	36	23 (16.79)	46
5.	Husband / family member	16 (9.82)	16	18 (13.14)	18
	Total	163 (100)	627	137 (100)	455

Figures in brackets are percentage to total.

Education of Children

Education is a crucial factor which determines the future of a person. Decisions concerning education of children are an important factor for measuring empowerment of women. Table 2 clearly exhibits the decision taken relating to education of children.

Table 2
Decision Making on Education of Children

Sl.No.	*Final Decision Taken*	*Public*		*Private*	
		Number of Respondents	*Total Score*	*Number of Respondents*	*Total Score*
1.	Self	84 (51.53)	420	58 (42.34)	290
2.	Myself more than husband /family member	32 (19.63)	128	29 (21.17)	87
3.	Both equal	28 (17.18)	84	18 (13.14)	54
4.	Husband / family member more than myself	14 (8.59)	28	20 (14.60)	40
5.	Husband / family member	5 (3.07)	5	12 (8.76)	12
	Total	163 (100)	665	137 (100)	483

Figures in brackets represent t-value.

It is observed from Table 2 that 51.53 per cent and 42.34 per cent of women in public and private sector respectively take decisions independently relating to children's education in their family. The percentages of women who jointly decide the education of their children in public and private sector are 45.4 and 48.91 respectively. The percentage of husband and family members taking decisions in this respect was 3.07 and 8.76 in the case of public and private sector respectively. Thus it is understood on the basis of total score value that the women in both sectors decide the education of their children independently.

Health and Medicine

Women have an important part to look after her family members' health. The details of decision making of women on health and medicines are furnished in Table 3.

It is deduced from Table 3 that nearly 14 per cent of the women working in public sector and about 23 per cent in private sector take independent decisions regarding health and medicine. Independent decision making was found more in private sector when compared to public sector. Joint decisions were taken by 58.90 per cent of families in the case of public sector while their percentage

Table 3
Decision Making on Health and Medicine

Sl.No.	*Final Decision Taken*	*Public*		*Private*	
		Number of Respondents	*Total Score*	*Number of Respondents*	*Total Score*
1.	Self	23 (14.11)	115	31 (22.63)	155
2.	Myself more than husband /family member	12 (7.36)	48	10 (7.30)	40
3.	Both equal	36 (22.09)	108	16 (11.68)	48
4.	Husband / family member more than myself	48 (29.45)	96	27 (19.71)	54
5.	Husband / family member	44 (26.99)	44	53 (38.69)	53
	Total	163 (100)	411 (100)	137 (100)	350 (100)

Figures in brackets represent t-value.

was 38.69 in private sector. Husband or family member alone taking decision was 26.99 per cent in public sector and 38.69 per cent in private sector. Thus, it is clear from the total score that majority of working women could take decisions independently regarding their health and medicine.

Leisure Activities

The leisure activities in families are another important factor of our life. The decision making on leisure activities are given in Table 4.

Table 4
Decision Making on Leisure Activities

Sl.No.	*Final Decision Taken*	*Public*		*Private*	
		Number of Respondents	*Total Score*	*Number of Respondents*	*Total Score*
1.	Self	92 (56.44)	460	63 (45.99)	189
2.	Myself more than husband /family member	48 (29.45)	192	31 (22.63)	93
3.	Both equal	11 (6.75)	33	26 (18.98)	78
4.	Husband / family member more than myself	7 (4.29)	14	10 (7.30)	20
5.	Husband / family member	5 (3.07)	10	7 (5.11)	7
	Total	163 (100)	709 (100)	137 (100)	387 (100)

Table 4 shows that 56.44 per cent and 45.99 per cent of women in public and private sector respectively take decisions independently regarding leisure activities in their family. When public sector is compared with private sector, independent decision making was found more in public sector. The percentages of women who jointly decide the leisure activities in public and private sectors are 40.49 and 48.91 respectively. The percentage of husband or family members taking decisions in this regard is 3.07 and 5.11 in the case of public and private sector respectively. Thus it is observed on the basis of total score value that working women decide the leisure activities in both public and private sectors.

It is inferred from the Table that 41.72 per cent in public sector and 40.15 per cent in private sector were in a position to purchase home appliances on their own decision. Joint decisions were taken by 49.09 per cent in the case of public sector and 46.72 per cent in private sector. Husband or family member alone taking decision rating to home appliance was 9.20 per cent and 13.14 per cent in public and private sector respectively. It is inferred from the analysis that joint decision was found to be dominant than than individual decision regarding the purchase of home appliances in the study area.

Table 5
Decision Making on Purchase of Home Appliances

Sl.No.	*Final Decision Taken*	*Public*		*Private*	
		Number of Respondents	*Total Score*	*Number of Respondents*	*Total Score*
1.	Self	68 (41.72)	340	55 (40.15)	275
2.	Myself more than husband /family member	36 (22.09)	144	27 (19.71)	108
3.	Both equal	28 (17.18)	84	21 (15.33)	63
4.	Husband / family member more than myself	16 (9.82)	32	16 (11.68)	32
5.	Husband / family member	15 (9.20)	15	18 (13.14)	18
	Total	163 (100)	615 (100)	137 (100)	496 (100)

Giving away Gifts

There is some sort of pleasure in giving and receiving gifts. As members of the society, we have to give gifts to others on many occasions like wedding, birthday and the like. It is a well-known fact that give and take policy enriches the friendship harmony, mutual help and the like among people. But women face a limitation in this respect. They cannot take independent decisions on most occasions without the consent of the men in their families. On many occasions, women are hesitant to attend social functions due to the lack of presents. Table 6 presents some interesting results of decision making on giving away gifts to others.

Table 6
Decision Making on Giving away Gifts to Others

SI.No.	*Final Decision Taken*	*Public*		*Private*	
		Number of Respondents	*Total Score*	*Number of Respondents*	*Total Score*
1.	Self	92 (56.44)	460	61 (45.53)	305
2.	Myself more than husband /family member	36 (22.09)	147	26 (18.98)	104
3.	Both equal	18 (11.04)	45	21 (15.33)	63
4.	Husband / family member more than myself	13 (7.98)	26	19 (13.87)	38
5.	Husband / family member	4 (2.45)	4	10 (7.30)	10
	Total	163 (100)	688 (100)	137 (100)	520 (100)

It is understood from the Table 6 that 56.44 per cent of women in public sector and 45.53 per cent in private sector could purchase and give gifts to others, according to their own decision. 41.11 per cent and 48.18 per cent of women in public and private sector respectively reported that they took the decisions jointly. It is observed during the survey that many women have said that if they had money, they would also be able to buy gifts for others.

Personal Needs

The details of decision making on personal needs of women are presented in Table 7.

Table 7 exhibits that 62.58 per cent of women working in public sector and 54.74 per cent working in private sector taking decision regarding their personal needs. The percentage of score value was less in private sector when compared to public sector decision making of women. 34.36 per cent of women working in public sector and 40.15 per cent of women working in private sector took decisions jointly. Only 3.07 per cent in public sector and 5.11 per cent in private sector had their decisions taken by husband and family members alone. Thus it may be inferred from the score value that majority of personal need decisions of women worker could be taken independently.

Table 7
Decision Making on Personal Needs

Sl.No.	*Final Decision Taken*	*Public*		*Private*	
		Number of Respondents	*Total Score*	*Number of Respondents*	*Total Score*
1.	Self	102 (62.58)	510	75 (54.74)	375
2.	Myself more than husband /family member	36 (22.09)	144	31 (22.63)	124
3.	Both equal	12 (7.36)	36	16 (11.68)	48
4.	Husband / family member more than myself	8 (4.91)	16	8 (5.84)	16
5.	Husband / family member	5 (3.07)	10	7 (5.11)	7
	Total	163 (100)	716	137 (100)	570

ANALYSIS OF ONE WAY ANOVA

In order to ascertain whether women working in different sectors have caused significant variation in empowerment scores, one way ANOVA test was carried out. The computed results of one way ANOVA for women work participants are given in Table 8.

Table 8
One Way Anova Test Results of Empowerment Scores among Women Work Participants

Source of Variation	*Degree of Freedom*	*Total Sum of Squares*	*Mean Square*	*F-Value*	$F_{0.05}$
Between groups	2	3531.86	1765.93	14.92*	3.00
Within groups	297	35152.92	118.66		
Total	299	38684.78			

* Significant at 5 per cent level.

The results presented in Table 8 revealed that there was a significant variation in empowerment scores between public and private sector women employees in the study area. Thus it may be concluded that the empowerment of women varied with different sectors among women workers.

LEVEL OF EMPOWERMENT

The empowerment of women has been classified into three levels namely low, medium, and high on the basis of average score value ($\bar{X}$) and its standard deviation (S.D). Table 9 reveals the level of empowerment of women work participants.

Table 9
Level of Empowerment of Women Work Participants

Sl.No.	Level of Empowerment	Public		Private	
		No. of Women Employees	Percentage	No. of Women Employees	Percentage
1.	High	94	57.67	66	48.17
2.	Medium	37	22.70	45	32.85
3.	Low	32	19.63	26	18.98
	Total	163	100.00	137	100

From the Table 9, it is clear that out of 163 sample women respondents in public sector, 94 (57.67 per cent) fall under high level empowerment, 37 (22.70 per cent) come under the category of medium level and 32 (19.63 per cent) fall under the low level. In the case of private sector, out of 137 respondents, 66 (48.17) of them belong to high level group, 45 (32.85 per cent) fall under medium level and remaining 26 (18.98 per cent) belong to low level.

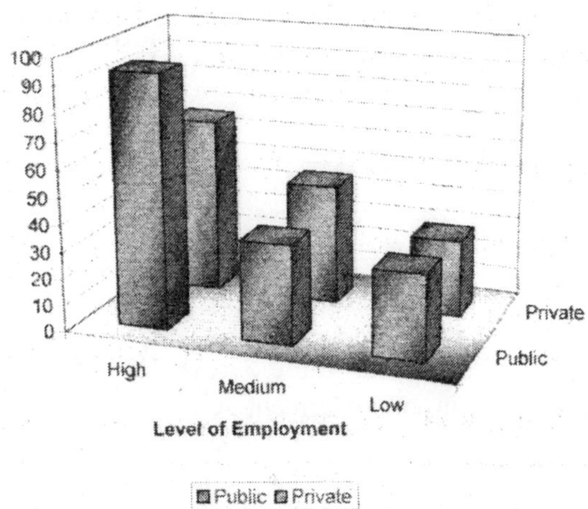

Figure 1: Level of Empowerment of Women Work Participation (in Numbers)

Relationship between the Level of Empowerment and Socio-Economic Factors of Women Work Participants

In order to examine the relationship between the level of empowerment and socio-economic factors like age, education, caste, family size, type of family, spouse employment and income, the chi-square test was carried out. The computed results are summarized in Table 10.

Table 10
The Result Chi-square Test between Level of Empowerment and Socio-economic Factors

Sl.No.		*Calculated Chi-square Value*	*Degree of Freedom*	*Table Chi-square Value at 5 per cent Level*	*Significance*
1.	Age	32.18	4	9.49	Significant
2.	Education	48.33	4	9.49	Significant
3.	Caste	1.004	2	5.99	Not Significant
4.	Family size	31.32	4	9.49	Significant
5.	Type of family	16.8921	2	5.99	Significant
6.	Spouse employment	8.471	2	5.99	Significant
7.	Income of respondent	21.48	4	9.49	Significant

It is inferred from Table 10 that the calculated Chi-square values for age, education, family size, type of family, spouse's employment and income of the respondents are greater than the table value of Chi-square at 5 per cent level of significance. Hence, there exists a relationship between these factors and level of empowerment. As the calculated value of Chi-Square is less than the table value at 5 per cent level in the case of caste, the caste has no influence on the level of employment of women in the study area.

ASSESSMENT OF CONTRIBUTION OF INDEPENDENT VARIABLES TO EMPOWERMENT

In order to assess the contribution of independent variables to women empowerment, stepwise multiple regression analysis was carried out. The results are presented in Table 11.

It is inferred from Table 11 that three of the variables were entered into the equation and the order of inclusion was as follows monthly

Table 11
Summary of Step Wise Multiple Regression
Dependent Variable Empowerment

Variables in Equation	*Multiple R*	R^2	*F*	*P*	*Beta*
Income	0.9612	0.92	137.12	0.01	0.96
Education	0.9748	0.94	113.78	0.01	0.32
Family Status (size)	0.9772	0.95	96.42	0.01	0.06

income, education and family status. It is observed from the results that as each of the additional variables was included, the values of multiple R and R^2 increased. It indicates that the income of the respondent, education and family status were the best set of predictors of empowerment of women having the combined contribution of about 95 per cent. Change in any one of the variables, while others kept constant, revealed that it was the income of the respondent which had the highest contribution to empowerment of women followed by education and family status respectively.

The findings of this chapter are summarized as follows.

The majority of the women work participants both public and private sectors were in a position to take independent decisions on all seven selected variables in the present study. The independent decision making capacity of women was found high in public sector than in private sector.

The results of ANOVA revealed that there was a significant variation in empowerment score between public and private sector. In the public sector, 57.67 per cent of sample women are having high level empowerment while it was only 48.17 per cent in public sector. The medium and low level were 22.70 per cent and 19.63 per cent respectively in public sector and it was 32.85 per cent and 18.98 per cent respectively in private sector.

The Chi-square test revealed that except caste of the respondents all other variables namely age, education, family size, type of family, spouse employment and income of the respondents were significantly related to the level of empowerment.

Step wise regression analysis revealed that the income of the respondents, education and family status were the best set of predictors of empowerment. Among these variables, income had a greater influence on women empowerment.

7

SUMMARY OF FINDINGS, CONCLUSIONS AND SUGGESTIONS

Women form the critical core input of the development of any economy. They contribute 2/3 of the world's work hours produce 50 per cent of world's food supplies, account for 60 per cent of the work force and contribute upto 30 per cent of the official labour force. The prosperity and balanced development of a country depends upon its women as they not only constitute nearly half of the population but have equally important role along with men in creating better life for the family. The role of women in economic development of our country is equally important as that of man. Woman's share in the labour force increased between 1970 and 2000. The new economy offers a plethora of opportunities to women. The post-reform period has been associated with growing employment opportunities for women. The participation of women in labour force is increasing in almost all the fields. The present study aims at analysing the role and participation of urban women in work force, their role in household decision making, quality of work life and empowerment.

The specific objectives of the study are

1. To study the relation between personal characteristics of women work participants and their familial characteristics.
2. To examine the variation in income between public and private sector women employees and assess the women workers contribution towards family income.
3. To analyse and compare the work-family conflict of women employees in public and private sector.

4. To assess the contribution of independent variables to quality of work life of women employees.
5. To analyse the extent to which women work participation empower them through decision making.
6. To examine the factors which influence the empowerment of working women in public and private sector.

The primary data required for the present study were collected from 300 sample women working in various offices both public and private sector through personal interview method. The survey was conducted from October 2001 to March 2002. The sample women employees were post-stratified into women working in public and private sector. Out of 300 sample women employees, 163 (54.33 per cent) belonged to public sector and remaining of 137 (45.67 per cent) came under private sector.

In the foregoing chapters, characteristics of the sample women employees, familial characteristics, contribution towards family income, work-family conflict, quality of work life, job satisfaction and empowerment of women have been discussed. The major findings along with conclusions and suggestions are now presented in this chapter.

SUMMARY OF FINDINGS

It was found that nearly 50 per cent of the sample women employees both in public and private sectors belonged to the age group of 30-40 years. Almost all the women employees were educated. About 90 per cent of the sample women employees were married. Unmarried and widows/divorcees were found to be below 5 per cent. Nearly 50 per cent of women employees both in public and private sectors asserted that the main reason for their taking up a job was to increase the family income followed by their desire to make use of their education. Majority of women employees (nearly 75 per cent) both in public and private sector earned Rs.5000 to Rs.10000 per month.

Regarding familial characteristics, nearly 75 per cent of women employees both in public and private sector belonged to Hindu religion followed by Christians in the study area. Nearly 80 per cent of women employees came from other castes followed by BC/MBC (13 to 14 per cent). About 60 per cent and 45 per cent of women employees working in public and private sector respectively have 3 to 5 members in their family. It is followed by below 3 members. Majority (nearly 80 per cent) of women employees were in joint family in both public and private sector. The spouses' monthly income was found higher for women employees working in public sector than private sector. It was observed that nearly 52 per cent and 59 per cent of public and private sector women employees respectively were earning a monthly family income of Rs.20,000-25,000.

In order to examine the relationship between the monthly income of the women employees and their family size, family monthly income, spouses' income, Chi-Square test was employed. The results revealed that a significant relation was found in family size, family income and spouses' income and monthly income of the women employees both in public and private sector.

Hypothesis 1: There is no variation in income among the women workers in public and private, central and state, and industry and service sectors.

ANOVA was applied to find the variation in monthly income between women employees working in different sectors. The result revealed that there was a significant variation in income among women employees working in public and private sector. It was also observed that there was a significant variation in income between Central and State Government employees under public sector and industry and service groups under private sector. Hence the hypothesis is proved.

The results of computed multiple regression model revealed that the earnings of women respondent and income of their spouses were statistically insignificant. It was understood that the contribution of women workers towards family income was not remarkable.

Regarding the work-family conflict, the analysis revealed the fact that the women employees in public sector were more deeply associated with family involvement, family expectations, work-family conflict and quality of work life compared to the women in private sector. Further it was observed that the Central Government employees were more closely associated with family involvement, family expectation, quality of work life and quality of family life than the State Government employees. In the case of private sector, women in industry were associated more with work involvement, family involvement, work family conflict and quality of work life than women in service category.

In the case of women employees in Central and State Government job, there was a negative and significant correlation between the variables work involvement, quality of work life and quality of family life. It reveals that any change in these variables may bring about negative involvement in work.

As far as women employees in private sector are concerned, any change in work conflict and family conflict effects changes in quality of work life in the opposite direction.

Hypothesis 2: There is no difference in the perception of quality of work life and job satisfaction between women workers in public and private sectors.

In order to examine the variations in perception of quality of work life (QWL), according to organisation and income, ANOVA was carried out. The results revealed that both public and private sector women employees differ significantly in the perception of quality of work life according to their income and types of organisations. Hence the hypothesis is proved.

Stepwise multiple regression analysis revealed that the job satisfaction had a greater contribution to quality of work life.

In order to measure the empowerment of women, 5 point scaling technique has been adopted. The women employees were classified into three categories namely low level, medium level and high level empowerment on the basis of empowerment score. In the public sector, 57.67 per cent of sample women were having high level empowerment while it was only 48.17 per cent in public sector. The medium and low level were 22.70 per cent and 19.63 per cent respectively in public sector and it was 32.85 per cent and 18.98 per cent respectively in private sector. Seven variables, namely (i) preparation of family budget, (ii) education of children, (iii) purchase of property, (iv) purchase of furniture, (v) purchase of house appliances, (vi) giving away gifts to others and (vii) personal needs were identified to assess the women empowerment through decision making in their family. The results revealed that almost all women employees in both public and private sectors were in a position to take independent decisions on all seven selected variables in the present study.

Hypothesis 3: There is no difference in women empowerment between public and private sector women employees.

In order to test the variation in empowerment in different sectors, ANOVA was carried out. The results revealed that there existed significant variation in empowerment between public and private sector women employees. Hence the hypothesis is proved.

To examine the relationship between socio-economic factors and level of empowerment, Chi-Square test was employed. It is inferred from the results that except caste of the respondents all other variables namely age, education, family size, type of family, spouse employment and income of the respondents were significantly related to the level of empowerment.

Stepwise regression analysis revealed that the income of the respondents, education and family status were the best set of predictors of empowerment. Among these variables, income had a greater influence on women empowerment.

CONCLUSION

With the acceptance of women and their participation in work force as a necessity, there is appreciation of their tremendous skills potentials. The participation of women in the work in the study area was intended not merely to improve their quality of life but to empower in decision making in their family. From the analysis of the empirical data, the women participation is found to be satisfactory. Higher level of internal consistency among women employees was observed in work involvement and quality of work life in the case of public sector. Thus it may be concluded that women employees in public sectors appeared much more satisfied in work force participation compared to private sector women employees.

In both public and private sector, women employees were in a positive frame of mind to take independent decisions which in turn ensured their empowerment in decision making in their family.

SUGGESTIONS

On the basis of the findings few tentative suggestions are offered which may help to enhance/ensure the participation of women in work force.

All efforts to promote participation initiatives can be viewed only in the context of economic independence and empowerment of women. Women in India are not able to contribute their best to the development of the society. It is because they are backward in education, and in social, economic and political spheres. Further, it is observed that the high incidence of illiteracy among women constituted one of the greatest barriers to their development. It limited their scope for work force participation. As such Government should take more efforts to promote women participation in work force. Women may be given equal opportunities for education, training, extension and decision making. Government can enact laws which ensures equal rights and opportunities for women with men in all job opportunities.

The study revealed that the performance of women employees in public sector was found to be satisfactory in all respects relating to the quality of work life and empowerment compared to private sector. Hence, conscious efforts have to be undertaken by the private sector organisations to promote women participation at a satisfactory level.

It is suggested that Government should promote exclusive organisations and programmes for women's participation. Government can support quasi-government, Pseudo-Governmental (co-operations), non-governmental and self-help groups for women. Further it is suggested that Government grants and aids may also be routed through exclusive women's organisations wherever they are prevailing.

The present study, for the many reasons outlined above, could be claimed to be opportune. India is a country with a hoary, mystery ancient culture that placed woman on a pedestal and glorified motherhood. But, the modern realities are quite different. Women have been at the receiving end. Male chauvinism and gender bias had often gone against the aspirations of women to play their true roles in society. It is in this context that a study that looks at the various options of women's empowerment that leads to her ultimate liberation, strikes the right note. The best is yet to be.

BIBLIOGRAPHY

BOOKS

Alagh Sharma, N. and Seema Singh (1993), *Indian Society of Labour Economics*, B.R.Publishing Conservation, Delhi, p. 380.

Amarjit Mahajan (1982), *Indian Police Women*, Deep and Deep Publication, New Delhi.

Andra Menefa Singh and A.D'Souza (1980), *The Urban Poor*, Manohar Publication, New Delhi.

Arrow, K.J. (1972), "Some Models of Racial Discrimination in the Labour Market", in Pascal (ed.) *Racial Discrimination in Economic Life*, Lexington, Mass: D.C. Health & Co.

Barron, B.D. and Norris, G.M. (1976), "Sexual Division and the Dual Labour Market", in Sheila and Barker (ed.), *Dependence and Exploitation in Work and Marriage*, London, Longmans.

Becker, G.S. (1975), *Human Capital*, Second Edition, New York: Columbia University Press.

Bohen, H., and Viveros-Long, A. (1981), *Balancing Jobs and Family Life*, Philadelphia: Temple University Press.

Devaki Jain (1975), *Indian Women*, Navajeevan Press, Ahamedabad, p. 74.

Edwards, R.C., Reich, M. and Gordon, D.M. (ed.) (1975), *Labour Market Segmentation*, Lexington Mass, D.C. Health & Co.

Hattery, Angela (2001), *Women Work and Family – Balancing and Weaving*, New Delhi, Sage Publications.

Hazel D'Lima (1983), *Women in Liocal Government*, Concept Publishing, New Delhi.

Indra Devi, M. (1987), *Women Education Employment: Family Living*, Granipale, New Delhi.

Jeyabalan (2001), *Women and Human Rights*, Atlantic Publishers and Distributors, New Delhi.

Kalarani (1976), *Role Conflict in Working Women*, Chetna Publications, New Delhi.

Kalpana Roy (1999), *Women and their Environment*, Rajah Publications, Vol. II, Delhi, p. 327.

Kothari, C.R. (1978), *Quantitative Techniques*, Vikas Publishing House Pvt. Ltd., New Delhi, p. 166.

Krishnamurthy, J. (1990), *Women in Colonial India*, Calcutta: Oxford University Press, p. 60.

Lalith Devi (1982), *Status and Employment of Women in India*, B.R. Publishing Corporation, Delhi.

Malthier, A. and Rogers, M. (1987), *Women and the Economy,* Macmillian, London, p. 58.

Mary Billington, F., *Women in India*, Air Marks Book Agency, New Delhi, pp. 9-11.

Margret Cormack (1976), *The Hindu Women*, Asia Publishing House, Bombay, p. 12.

Mayashah (1982), *Theories of Segmented Labour Market in Essays on Recent Developments in Economics*, Department of Economics, University of Baroda, Baroda.

Misra Savara (1986), *Changing Trends in Women's Empty – A Case Study of the Taxable Industry in Bombay*, Himalaya Publishing House, Bombay.

Murali Manohar, K. (1989), *Socio-Economic Status of Indian Women*, Mittal Publications, Delhi, p. 115.

Peterfallon and Donald, V. (1988), *The Economics of Labour Markets*, Oxford: Phillip Allan.

Pleck, J. (1984), "*The Work-family Role System, Work and Family: Changing Roles of Men and Women*. In P. Voydanoff (ED.), *Work and Family Palo Alto*, CA: May field.

Pleck, J. (1985), "*Working Wives/Working Husbands*", Beverly Hills, CA: Sage Publication.

Premilla Kapur (1974), *The Changing Status of Working Women in India*, Vikas Publication, New Delhi.

Ruddar Datt and K.P.M. Sundaram (2003), *Indian Economy*, S. Chand & Company Ltd., New Delhi, p. 419.

Rani Moses (1992), *Dalits and Women*, Gurukal Summer Institute, Chennai, pp. 197-198.

Singh, K.P. (1979), *Status of Women and Population, Growth in India*, Munishiram Manoharlal, New Delhi.

Stephen Pictchnis, G. (1975), *The Canadian Labour Market*, (Toronto: Oxford University Press, p. 228.

Subba Rao, P. (2000), *Human Resource Management in the New Millennium*, Himalaya Publishing House, Delhi, pp. 6-7.

JOURNALS

Anju Grover (2002), "Gender Equity – A View", *Southern Economist*, Vol. 40, No. 18, January 15, p. 26.

Annupa Gupta (1971), "The Problems of Working Women", *Yojana*, Vol. XV, No. 4 and 5, March 21, p. 21.

Azad Singh Gulab (1988), "Development of Entrepreneurship among Rural Women – An Overview", *Small Enterprises Development Management and Extension*, Vol. XV, June, p. 44.

Banerjee Nirmala (1985), "Modernisation and Marginalisation", *Social Scientist,* Vol. 13, October-November, pp. 48-71.

Bhanumathi Vasudevan (1992) "Defining Women in the Work Place", *HRD Newsletter*, April-June, p. 7.

Burke, R. and Weir, T. (1976), "Relationship of Wives' Employment Status to Husband, Wife and Pair Satisfaction and performance", *Journal of Marriage and The Family*, Vol. 38, pp. 279-287.

Chandhury, R.K. (1987), Supply of Work Effort by Women in India - How Equal is their Contribution to Benefit Sharing? Conference, *Volume of the Indian Economic Association*, Seventieth Annual Conference, Jaipur.

Chin Lee Gan (1988), "Economic Theories of Women's Inferior Labour Market Position", *Indian Journal of Economics*, 19(272): 06-11.

Cohen, M.S. (1971), "Sex Differences in Compensation", *Journal of Human Resources*, Vol. 6, p. 485.

Desai, and D. Jain (1994), "On Women's Work in Rural India", *Population Development Review*, Vol. 20(1), pp. 115-136.

Economic Affairs, Vol. 41, Qn. 3, Sep 1996, p. 187.

Fisher, C.C. (1987), "Toward a more Complete Understanding of Occupational Sex Discrimination", *Journal of Economic Issues*, 21(1): 113-139.

Gangrade, K.D. (1993), "Women and Child Workers in Unorganised Sector", *Indian Journal of Labour Economics*, Vol. 36, No. 4, p. 11.

Greenhnauns, J. and Beutell, N. (1985), "Sources of Conflict between Work and Family Roles", *Academy of Management Review*, Vol. 10, pp. 76-88.

Joshi Rama, J. (1988), "Women Cur Work: Implication for Organisation", *Indian Journal of Industrial Relations*, 23(4), April, pp. 461-480.

Kalpana Sharma (1988), "Women in Perspective", *Indian Express*, July 31, p. 8.

Kamala Nath (1970), "Female Work Participation and Economic Development", *Economic and Political Weekly*, Vol. 5, No. 21, May 23, p. 846.

Kelly, R. and Voydanoof, P. (1985), "Work-Family Role Strain among Employed Parents", *Family Relations*, Vol. 34, pp. 367-374.

Kopelman, R., Greenhaus, J. and Connolly, T. (1983), "A Model of Work Family and Interrole Conflict, a Construct Validation Study", *Organisational Behaviour and Human Performance*, Vol. 38, pp. 198-215.

Krishnaj, N. (1995), "Working Mothers and Child Survival in Rural India: Insights from Special Pattern", *Economic and Political Weekly*, November, pp. 2803-2808.

Lawrence Marry (1996), "Status of Working Women", *Kisan World*, Vol. 23, No. 12, December, p. 34.

Levitan, T., Quinn, R. and Staines, G.L. (1971), "Sex Discrimination Against the American Working Women", *American Behavioral Scientist*, Vol. 15, p. 242.

Linda Elizabeth Duxbury and Christopher Alan Higgins (1991), "Gender differences in Work-Faminly Conflict", *Journal of Applied Psychology*, Vol. 76, No. 1, pp. 60-74.

Linda Mayoux (1998), "Participatory Learning for Women's Empowerment in Micro Finance Programmes: Negotiating, Complexity, Conflict and Change", *IDS Bulletin*, Vol. 29, No. 4, pp. 39-50.

Madhu Kishwar (1985), "Gandhi on Women", *Economic and Political Weekly*, October 5, pp. 88-91.

Mehta, G.S. (1989), "Education, Employment and Earnings; of the Extent of Disadvantages Against Women", *Man and Development*, Vol. XI, No. 2, June, pp. 20-34.

Mother Terasa Women's University (1982), "A Study on Status of Women in Kodaikanal", *The Hindu*, Feb-12, p. 17.

Muehlberger U. (2000), "Women's Labour Force Attachment in Europe: An Analytical Framework and Empirical Evidence for the Household, IRISS, C/I, Working Papers.

Nirmala Banerjee (1989), "Trend in Women's Employment – Some Macro Level Observations", *Economic and Political Weekly*, April, pp. 71-81.

Patel, B.B. and Dholakka, Ravinder, H. (1978), "Female Labour Force Participation Rate: Direct Verification of Some Hypothesis", *Indian Journal of Labour Economics,* January.

Pleck, J. (1977), "The Work-family Role System", *Social Problems*, Vol. 24, 1977, pp. 417-428.

Pleck, J. (1979) "Work-Family Conflict; A National Assessment", *Paper Presented of the Annual Meeting of the Society for the Study of Social Problems*, Boston.

Prabhai Rai (1975), "Women Labour-Uniform Discrimination", *Yojana*, May, p. 18.

Radha Devi and M.Ravidran (1985), "Working Women and Household Work", *Social Change*, Vol. 15, No. 2, June.

Radha Krishna Rao (2001), "Kerala Model of Women's Empowerment", *Social Welfare*, Vol. 47, No. 11, pp. 35-41.

Sekaran, V. (1983), "Factors Influencing the Quality of Life in Dual-career Families", *Journal of Occupational Psychology*, Vol. 56, pp. 161-174.

Sennoh-Muller, L. (1990), "Growing Old in Latin America", *World Health*, April-May, p. 13.

Shamir, B. and Salomon, J. (1985), "Work-at-home and the Quality of Working Life", *Academy of Management*, Vol. 10, pp. 455-464.

Shakuntala Balaraman (1986), "Women Image Making and Shaping – Over Throwing Stereotypes", (Book Review), *Economic and Political Weekly*, October, p. 31.

Shaul S., Marine (1982), "The Status of Women in Local Governments", *An International Assessment*, November-December.

Shoma Chatterjee (1990), "Women in Management: An Uphill Task", *The Economic Times*, June 13, p. 8.

Staines, G., Plectk, J., Shepard, L. and O' Connor, P. (1978), "Wives' Employment Status and Marital Adjustment: Yet Another Look", *Psychology of Women Quarterly*, Vol. 3, pp. 90-120.

Strandt Kathleen (1986), "Women Development and the State–On the Theoretical Impasse", *Development and Change*, Vol. 17, No. 21, April, p. 105.

Sumit Gupta and Mukta Gupta (1989), "Women in India: Retrospect and Prospect", *Women's World*, No. 21-22, pp. 4-5

Terborg, J.R. and Illgen, D.R. (1975), "Sex Discrimination and Sex-role Stereo types: Are they Synonymous?", *Organisation Behaviour and Human Performance*, No. 12: 154-57.

Yogev, S. and Brett, J., "Pattern of Work ad Family Involvement among Single and Dual-Earner Couples", *Journal of Applied Psychology*, Vol. 70, pp. 754-786.

REPORTS

Assistant Executive Engineer, Public Works Department, Srivaikuntam. Office of the Assistant Director of Statistics, Chidambaranar District, Thoothukudi, March, 1992.

Documentation on Women and Children, July-December, 1998, p. 23.

Jeyalakshmi, D. (1986), "Development of Women and the Impact of Higher Secondary Education", *Report of the Workshop on Development of Women* through Ed 7. Mother Teresa Women's University, Kodaikanal, April 2-3.

Ramachandran, P. (1964), *Attitudes of Women in Part Time Employment*, Part I – Report, Department of Social Research, Tata Institute of Social Sciences, Bombay, (Mimeographed).

Ranade, S.N. and Ramachandian (1970), *Women and Employment Reports of Pilot Studies Conducted in Delhi*, Bombay, T.I.S.S. Bombay.

Sharaya Mhatre (1978) *Women in Banking*, Unpublished Report, Bombay National Institute of Bank Management, p. 21.

"Structural Changes in the Employment of Women (1971-1981), An analysis of the Changing Distribution of Women's Employment", *Quarterly Economic Report of India Institute of Public Opinion*, Vol. XXX, No. 1, Mar-Aug, 1986, pp. 24-33.

Zachariah, K.C. (1994), *Demographic Transition in Kerala in the 1980's*. CDS Monograph Series, Trivandrum, 1994.

THESIS

Unwalla, J.N. (1977), *Study of Women Executives at Work and at Home*. An unpublished Ph.D thesis, Tata Institute of Social Sciences, Bombay.

WEBSITE

Ota, Yoshie (1999), Women in the Labour Force in Japan, Challenges and Opportunities for the New Millennium. *http//www.us.japan.org/society* feature.

21-24 / 30/8/10 Im-2957 / 13/8/10 SBS 2 copy / 5 copy

OK